The Brain Explained

Daniel Drubach, MD

Department of Neurology
University of Maryland
School of Medicine
Baltimore, MD

Prentice Hall Health, Upper Saddle River, NJ 07458

Publisher: Julie Alexander
Editor in Chief: Cheryl Mehalik
Acquisitions Editor: Mark Cohen
Senior Production Editor: Janet Bolton
Production Manager: Patrick Walsh
Director of Production/Manufacturing: Bruce Johnson
Prepress/Manufacturing Buyer: Ilene Sanford
Director of Marketing: Leslie Cavaliere
Marketing Manager: Kristin Walton
Advertising Coordinator: Cindy Frederick
Art Director: Marianne Frasco
Interior Design: Robin S. Hall
Interior Art: Biruta Akerbergs Hansen
Cover Design: Miguel Ortiz
Cover Art: Biruta Akerbergs Hansen
Full-Service Production/Composition: Publishers' Design and Production
    Services, Inc.
Printer/Binder: Banta Harrisonburg

Printed in the United States of America

10   9   8   7   6   5   4   3   2   1

ISBN: 0-13-796194-4

Prentice-Hall International (UK) Limited, *London*
Prentice-Hall of Australia Pty. Limited, *Sydney*
Prentice-Hall Canada Inc., *Toronto*
Prentice-Hall Hispanoamericana, S.A., *Mexico*
Prentice-Hall of India Private Limited, *New Delhi*
Prentice-Hall of Japan, Inc., *Tokyo*
Prentice-Hall (Singapore) Pte., Ltd.
Editora Prentice-Hall do Brasil, Ltda., *Rio de Janeiro*

Contents

Introduction

I am a big fan of brains in general and of my brain in particular. There are so many things that one can do with a brain, it's hard to imagine what one would do without one. Brains are like good friends: Not only are they nice to have, but in fact, they are pretty much indispensable. Rather than an optional commodity, brains are very much a necessity for a pleasant and successful life. Yet most people go through life without giving their brains much thought. In my opinion, this is a serious mistake.

I've created this book to help you gain insight into the functions and dynamics of the most fascinating and complex commodity that each of us possesses. It interjects discussions of complex concepts with humor, anecdotes, philosophical discussions and clinical case studies, and covers a significant amount of updated subject matter plus material rarely found in standard neuroanatomy and neurophysiology texts—such as brain plasticity, dreaming, consciousness, and aggression. I hope that this book will help you to understand the "big picture" behind the functions of the brain by integrating data from the realms of basic sciences, psychology, psychiatry, and neurology.

INTENDED AUDIENCE

This has been designed as a supplementary text on neuroscience for students in such allied health fields as nursing, social work, psychology, and the rehabilitation disciplines, including physical, occupational, recreational and speech and language therapies. It may also have some appeal for lay readers.

KEY FEATURES

- Provides a "holistic" approach to the study of the brain, interpreting knowledge from the fields of neurology, psychiatry, psychology, and basic sciences.

- Goes beyond discussions on the morphology and physiology of the brain by presenting the central nervous system as what it is: not only a group of neurons and lobes, but an extremely complex, integrated system responsible for an extraordinarily wide scope of functions.
- Offers an entertaining, conversational and easy-to-read narrative style, using analogies, metaphors, and humor.

REVIEWERS

Glenn Labrozzi, PT
Director, Physical Therapist Assistant Program
Mercyhurst College
Erie, PA

Eydie Kendall
Academic Coordinator of Clinical Education
North Idaho College
Coeur d'Alene, ID

Harriet Conley Wichowski
Assistant Professor, Nursing
University of Wisconsin–Green Bay
Green Bay, WI

1 Overview of Functions of Your Product

Your brain is the foundation of your being. Without your own particular brain, you would not be you. People can undergo heart, liver, or kidney transplants and continue to have the same psychological and spiritual make-up as before; in essence, they continue to be themselves. But since the brain contains the very essence of who you are, a brain transplant would turn you into a totally different individual.

Your brain is not a particularly handsome organ (unlike you, my dear reader); it pretty much looks like a wrinkled, dried-out prune. It is also not especially big; it weighs only about 3 pounds. Yet you would be lost without your brain. As small and ugly as it is, your brain can do an extraordinary number of things for you. Let's summarize what we can do with our brains.

RECEIVE INFORMATION

The brain receives and processes information about the universe surrounding an individual. Through a person's eyes, the brain receives visual information; through the ears, auditory input; through the nose, olfactory data; through receptors in the skin, details about touch; and through taste buds in the tongue, taste information. All this may seem straightforward, but we must remember that after receiving this information, the brain must then process and make sense of it. Thus, if I see my mother-in-law's face, the brain must interpret the visual image as that of a face and subsequently recognize it as the face of my mother-in-law. The brain will also immediately associate the image with all the information it has stored about my mother-in-law (how nice a person she is and how much I love her). In addition, from some particular features present today on her face, my brain will deduct that she is, as usual, angry at me. All of this activity—registering an image (light beams with a particular pattern), searching its memory storage to associate the image with a particular object (a face and, afterward, that of my mother-in-law, and even more particular, my angry mother-in-law), and registering memory stores to retrieve all that is known about that particular face (remembering how much I love her, which is termed *affective coloring*—is done by the brain within a minuscule fraction of a second, too minuscule for humans to be able to measure.

We will learn in this manual that specific areas of the brain are responsible for each of the steps involved in the recognition of my well-loved but angry mother-in-law, and that a lesion in any of these areas or in the connections between them will result in a number of clinical syndromes. For example, a patient of mine who suffered trauma to the head from a surfboard accident could identify the pattern of a face as a face but failed to recognize who the face belonged to, even if it was that of his son, wife, or mother. Only when the person who the face belonged to spoke was he be able to identify it. The connections between the areas of the brain responsible for pattern recognition (identifying a face, or *prosopagnosia*) and the area of memory storage for identifying particular faces were affected by the accident.

This function of receiving and processing information is incredibly complex. To illustrate this point, take as a seemingly simple example the word *ocean*. The brain associates the word *ocean* with the image of an ocean, whether the word is written in printed or cursive characters or whether it is heard after being spoken by children or adults (in voices that could have thousands of different sound pitches or accents) or whether it is felt by the fingers on a relieved surface. One could program a computer to associate the written or spoken word *ocean* with a picture of an ocean, but one could not possibly program the most sophisticated computer in the world to be able to recognize all of the possible variations on the word, which the brain is able to identify and associate with the concept of an ocean.

An interesting question that arises and that we discuss in more detail later is the following: When a group of people look at the same object, do they all perceive the same thing? In subsequent chapters, we learn that receptive organs in the body, such as the eyes and ears, change, or *transduce*, one type of energy, such as light beams or sound waves, into a second sort of energy, electrochemical impulses. As we will discover, the brain's essential form of operation is through these electrochemical processes. Our brain is not like a mirror that reflects exact images of what our eyes perceive, but it transduces this *visual image* into a *mental representation* consisting of electrochemical patterns with which it can work. Could there be individual differences in this mental image? Could the perception of the universe be unique to each individual? We can never get an answer to this question because as with the phenomenon of dreams, we are unable to see the mental image that another person sees. Jewish sages of many centuries ago declared, "Even as men's faces are not alike, so their understanding (or perception) is not alike. Each man has an understanding that is his very own." Our very own perception of reality is hidden from all others. Only we perceive what we perceive. This may account for differences in such things as taste or appreciation of beauty among individuals.

ACT ON THE EXTERNAL UNIVERSE

The brain is also responsible for the motor output that allows the individual to act upon and interact with the external universe. Thus, it controls all types of movement, which is the way that we act upon the universe around us. A totally immobile individual, one who is unable to move any of his limbs or facial muscles, would not be able, under usual circumstances, to act upon the world around him. The brain thus controls walking, working with the hands, smiling, crying, playing a musical instrument (that talent is not in the hands; it is in the brain), facial expression, and other forms of body language. In an unfortunate neurological condition resulting from a certain lesion in the brainstem, disconnecting the brain from all of the body's muscles, the individual can become "locked in," a prisoner within his own body. The individual's mentation is normal; he can smell, hear, and see the world around him, but he cannot communicate with it, although some patients with this disorder can communicate to some degree with their eyes.

UTILIZE LANGUAGE

What would you do without words? Think of the word "universe." It encompasses the trees, the raindrops, the stars, the animals, the oceans, the people. If it wasn't for the word, how would it be possible for a person to contain everything within the universe in the space occupied by a mere eight letters? Words have enormous power. They are not mere combinations of letters. They are the means by which we think, and they contain everything in the universe within ourselves. Language, the utilization of words and other symbols for encasing objects and ideas, is one of the most advanced functions of the brain.

POSSESS EMOTIONS

The brain is responsible for the affective universe within us, for all of our emotions and feelings. It controls love, hate, our sense of beauty, anger, rage, moods, and feelings of pleasure and displeasure (love is not in the heart, it's actually in the brain). It attaches *affective coloring*, that is, it adds affective meaning to meaningful objects and experiences. Thus, lesions in the brain can dramatically change the way people behave, their personalities, their moods. Certain lesions can make normally violent people become placid and nonviolent, and vice versa. One of my patients, a painter who suffered a stroke, found his paintings no longer beautiful, which led to a change in his whole style of painting. Another patient, who suffered trauma to the brain from a boating accident, became far more pleasant with his family, who he had previously abused both verbally and physically. His wife and children were delighted with the change, leading to a much healthier family life. A normally somber funeral director became exceedingly jovial after a head injury, breaking out laughing at unusual times during the day, including while conducting funerals. As can be expected, this unusual behavior was not conducive to a successful business, and he was delegated to directing traffic in the home's parking lot. Other people who suffer brain injuries can become more aggressive, or decisive, or explosive, or they may lose or gain motivation and drive, becoming more or less physically or mentally active.

COGNITION

The brain is responsible for our cognitive processes, that is, our memory, intelligence, and thoughts. It is the source of our creativity, our ability to learn information and use that information to control our behavior. It is responsible for our ability to solve problems, to plan behavior and activities, to respond appropriately to situations encountered from minute to minute during our lives. It analyzes information, separates the necessary from the unnecessary, the truth from the untruth. It is responsible for all of the complex psychological functions that make us human, and among humans, who each of us is as an individual.

CONTROL THE BODY'S ENDOCRINE SYSTEM

The brain controls the endocrine system, influencing basically all the hormone-secreting glands in our bodies. By means of its control over the thyroid, suprarenal, and other glands, the brain affects such processes as our metabolic rate, balance of weight, and blood pressure. In women it regulates the menstrual cycle, ovulation, and lactation after childbirth. This interaction between the brain and the endocrine system explains the connection between psychological factors and "hormonal" processes. Thus, depression can affect, among other things, menstruation, ovulation, sex drive, and weight.

CONTROL OF AUTONOMIC FUNCTIONS

The brain is in control of the autonomic functions, that is, all of our bodily functions that are necessary to maintain homeostasis and life. The brain influences heart rate, blood pressure, intestinal motility, rate of sweating, rate of breathing, and other things that you should be glad you do not have to worry about. Imagine what life would be like if you constantly had to remember to keep the sphincters in your bladder contracted all the time until you decided go to the bathroom and relax them!

CONTROL OF IMMUNITY

The brain also has an important function in the control of immunity, in the body's defenses against infections and malignancies. This is a fascinating subject that has generated much research in recent years.

DO ALL OF THE ABOVE SIMULTANEOUSLY

Above anything else, the brain is responsible for integrating all of the functions described above. More on this subject appears in subsequent chapters, but to illustrate this point, consider the following example: A concert pianist is about to give a concert. His brain directs his legs to walk to the piano. As he walks, he hears noise patterns that the brain interprets as applause. He recognizes among his public seated in the first row the face of his son. The warm and proud feeling he gets when he looks at his child results from the affective areas of his brain imparting affective coloring to the image of his son. As he prepares to play the first piece, he becomes slightly nervous, which causes the area of the brain that controls autonomic function to raise his blood pressure and heart rate as well as to produce stomach contraction, which results in the feeling of tightness in his stomach. When his hands touch the piano keys, his brain searches in the memory stores for the notes of the music he is about to play. As he begins playing, the area responsible for auditory information in his brain detects that his playing is too fast and sends information to areas responsible for movement to slow his hands.

2 Structure of the Brain

Before describing in more detail what your brain looks like, we will discuss the building blocks that make up the brain: the brain cells.

THE LITTLE PICTURE: BRAIN CELLS

You, my distinguished reader, are a living, breathing paradox. On the one hand, you are One, a whole, unrepeatable, unique, and indivisible entity, unamenable to being broken into more than one unit. On the other hand, you are more than one. Your self is actually the aggregation of billions and billions of individual tiny living units that are called *cells*.

Cells are miniature organisms that contain all necessary functions to maintain life. Like all organisms, cells are born, live, and die. The life activity of most cells in the body can be compared to the actions of an individual human being in a society. In essence, most cells and humans perform three types of function. The first type consists of functions necessary to maintain one's body and to grow. This includes feeding, performing daily maintenance and care, eliminating waste, and seeking to make the environment around oneself a pleasant one. The second type of function directly or indirectly helps society, such as holding a job and performing certain community activities. Every cell in the body has such a job: cells of the heart pump blood to every organ; stomach cells produce enzymes to digest food necessary for survival; liver and kidney cells help process and eliminate waste that would otherwise be toxic to all other organs. The third type of function is reproduction. Most cells in your body maintain the ability to reproduce after you are born, although some cells, such as those in muscle, may do so only when the original cells become damaged.

All of the cells in your body have one common goal: your survival. Each cell has a specific function to fulfill that goal. In order to perform its highly specific activity, cells throughout the body take on certain physical and functional characteristics that make them adept at performing their jobs.

Brain matter contains two types of cells, which compose a two-tier class system. *Neurons* are the elite class, the "kings and queens," the stars of the brain, responsible for all of the functions described in the prior chapter. They are the cells in charge of thinking, feeling, hearing, seeing, moving, loving, and hating.

The other type of cells of the brain are *glial cells*, which are the "attendant" class, but their role is so vital to the survival of neurons that they are the unsung heroes of the brain. After all, what king can sustain his kingship with servants? The main purpose of glial cells is to cater to and fulfill all of the needs of neurons. Glial cells are responsible for creating the ideal environment in which neurons can live, grow, and work comfortably. Glial cells are described in more detail in subsequent sections.

NEURONS

Neurons are fascinating cells. As opposed to many other cells in the body, neurons perform only two of the cell functions described above. They carry out activities to maintain themselves and their community (you), but they do not reproduce. In fact, at birth a person has the largest number of neurons that he or she will ever have; from then on their number decreases (which means that you really have to take care of the ones you have). Why this is so is unknown, but some neuroscientists have theorized that neurons are so busy taking care of themselves and performing a job (very much like some hard-driven career individuals) that they have no time to reproduce.

This being said, recent research has demonstrated that under very rare conditions, such as with the use of certain pharmacological agents, and in a very limited fashion, a small number of neurons are born after an individual is born and even at a later age, but the reason and purpose for those neurons are not well understood.

Structure of Neurons

Neurons are funny-looking creatures. They can take many shapes, but your typical neuron looks like a weird space alien with a fat triangular body and a round head (the nucleus) inside it (Figure 2-1). The nucleus is the "brain" of the cell. Emerging from the body and other areas are multiple short, skinny arms called *dendrites*, which reach out to other neurons to receive information. From the cell's body also emerges one long foot or tail (the axon), which can be several inches to several feet long and which branches out at the end, where it connects with other cells to which it conveys information. The axon works very much like a one-way wire, transmitting impulses away from the body of the neuron and never toward it. Also very much like a wire, axons are covered on all sides by an insulating

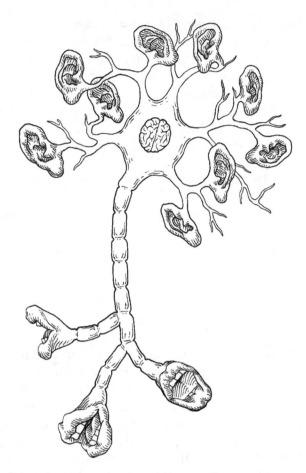

FIGURE 2-1   Schematic representation of a typical neuron. Notice the cell body and the dendrites reaching out to receive (or "hear") messages from other neurons. The axon emerges from the cell body and can be several feet long. It ends at the presynaptic area (represented by "mouth"), which communicates information to other neurons.

material called *myelin*, which allows nerve impulses to travel at a faster speed, and, as we see later, they are involved in many diseases of the brain.

Neurons are islands in a sea of liquid called *extracellular fluid*, which surrounds them from all sides; although close to each other, neurons, for the most part, do not touch.

Function of Neurons

There are no spare neurons, no reserve cells in the brain. Every single neuron in the nervous system has a particular function. They are highly specialized technicians; most neurons perform one (and only one) specific activity and do it extremely well. Thus, certain neurons are specialized in processing visual information, others in understanding spoken language, yet others in deciphering written information or in interpreting and expressing emotions or feelings. Neurons with the same specialization and a common function to perform gang up in groups in specific areas of the brain, as we explore when we talk about localization of brain functions later in this chapter. Thus, every function of the brain, such as processing language, movement, sensation and so on, are carried out by groups of neurons with a common purpose and located in the same general area of the brain. The number of neurons in each group varies widely.

Not all neurons are created equal. In fact, the brain is like a planet, containing many populations of neurons, each with distinctive physical and functional characteristics (Figure 2-2). There are wide variations among these populations, including variations in size, shape, manner in which they process information, and neurotransmitters (chemical messengers, described shortly) that they use to communicate with other neurons. There are even differences in the vulnerability to noxious influences. For

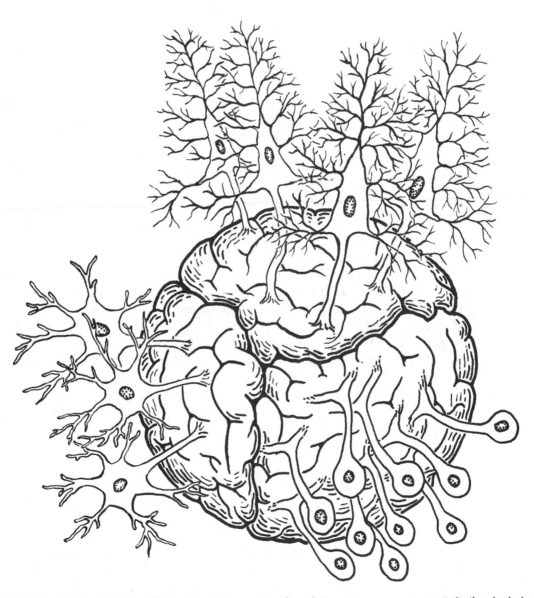

FIGURE 2-2 The brain planet. The brain contains a number of populations of neurons, each with distinctive physical and functional characteristics. Size and shape of individual neurons vary widely among these populations.

example, some neurons in areas of the brain such as the cerebellum and the limbic system (described in later sections) are very vulnerable to low levels of oxygen. They are much more likely to become damaged in cases of cardiac arrest when the delivery of oxygen to the brain is interrupted. Neurons with a common localization in the brain and a common function to perform tend to belong to the same population and have common physical and functional characteristics.

In general, neurons in an adult human brain are so physically and functionally adept at performing their particular functions that they are not at all interchangeable. That is to say, a neuron with the function of processing auditory information is not capable, even if surgically transplanted to other areas of the brain, of processing visual information. However, neuroscientists have made an important discovery in recent years: When neurons with a particular function are damaged by a disorder such as a stroke, there is some scientific evidence that *neighboring* neurons with a different function are capable, to a very limited extent, of taking on the functions of the damaged neurons. This process is especially effective in infants. As an individual gets older, this process becomes less effective. This issue is discussed in greater detail in the section on brain plasticity.

Each neuron also works as a team with the rest of the neurons. In fact, teamwork among neurons is the essence of brain function. This is particularly impressive if we consider that there are approximately 100 billion neurons in the brain. One hundred billion of anything is impressive, but when we think that each neuron has a specific function and that it connects with approximately 1000 other neurons in the performance of this function, the fact that neurons function as a team is particularly mind boggling.

In spite of the incredible complexity of the functions of the brain, the main function of individual neurons, besides those pertaining to maintaining their health, is to communicate with other neurons. This process of communication involves three steps: receiving a signal, processing it, and sending the signal on to other neurons. Thinking, talking, running, loving, seeing, and feeling are all the result or the cause of communication within neurons.

In fact, most scientists believe that all human activities related to functions of the brain, such as language, thought, emotions, and movement, are the product of activation and communication among populations of neurons. If neurons responsible for a particular activity become "silent," that is, unable to communicate with other neurons, that activity cannot take place.

Communication within Neurons

Communication within neurons occurs through an electrochemical process that involves both electricity and chemical substances called *neurotransmitters*. Neurotransmitters are manufactured within neurons and are utilized by them to communicate with other neurons. You can think of them as the chemical words or language utilized by neurons to communicate with each other. Under normal conditions, neurons can communicate within themselves only by means of neurotransmitters.

Dozens of neurotransmitter have been identified, and the list grows larger every year. We discussed that the brain contains a variety of populations of neurons, each with distinctive physical and functional features. As is the case with populations within our planet that are able to speak and understand a particular language, each population of neurons manufactures and responds to one or more select neurotransmitters, and it is unable to manufacture or respond to those with which it has not been predetermined to communicate. Thus, groups of neurons that have the same function (such as processing language) and belong to the same population manufacture and communicate through the same neurotransmitter.

Most neurotransmitters are manufactured within neurons from raw products that are imported from the outside of the neuron. In essence, neurons act like a neurotransmitter manufacturing plant. The chemical workers carrying on the work are called *enzymes*. In order for the components of the manufacturing process to proceed in an efficient manner, the neuron contains an extensive and highly sophisticated transport mechanism to transport substances from one area of the neuron to another and from the outside to the inside of the neuron, and vice versa (Figure 2-3). We deal with this subject in more detail in subsequent chapters, but it is important to point out that the effective transport of neurotransmitters

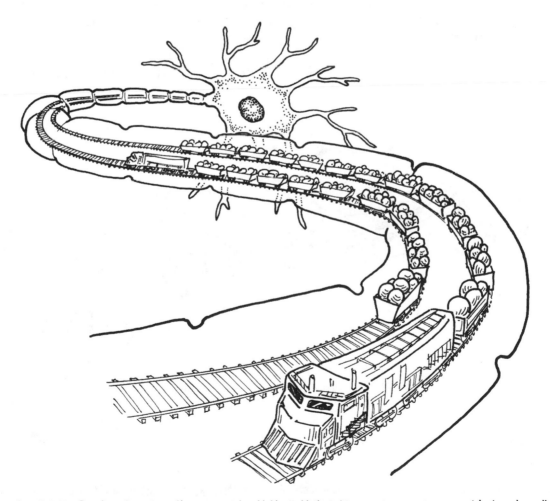

FIGURE 2-3   Axonal transport. Neurons contain a highly sophisticated transport system to move nutrients and supplies through various areas of the neuron.

within the neuron is of utmost importance for effective transmission. Certain neurological disorders will alter the transport mechanism in neurons, interfering with the transport of substances within different areas of the cell. Such is the case with a process called "diffuse axonal injury," which is seen in patients who suffer traumatic brain injury. It is thought that mechanical forces brought on by the injury "stretch" the axon, which will result in damage to the mechanism of transport between the cell body and the axon. This alteration in transport could potentially lead to neuronal death (Figure 2-4).

After manufacture by the neuron, neurotransmitters are stored in pouches called *vesicles*. Aside from providing convenient storage sites, vesicles serve to prevent destruction of the neurotransmitter molecules by enzymes that are present in the intracellular fluid within the neuron.

Any process of communication between two beings involves the transmission of a message by one entity and the reception and correct interpretation of that message by the receiving entity. The same applies to communication between neurons. But how and where does the communication take place? We indicated that neurons are like islands, having no physical contact between each other, but the area where they are closest to each other and where communications between them occurs is called the *synapse* (Figure 2-5). The synapse is actually a space between the end of the axon of the neuron sending the message (the *presynaptic neuron*) and the dendrite or other parts of the membrane of the neuron receiving the message (the *postsynaptic neuron*) (Figure 2-6).

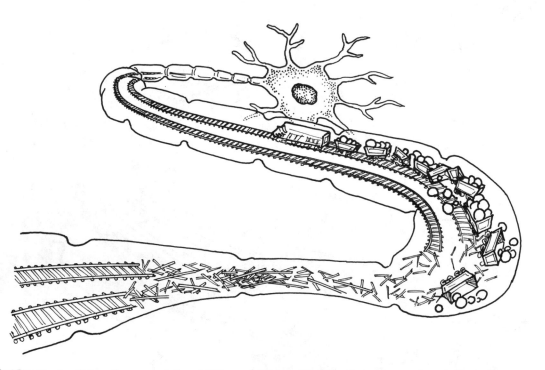

FIGURE 2-4   Schematic representation of diffuse axonal injury. Stretching forces damage the axonal transport mechanism, affecting the transport of substances between the cell body and more distal parts of the axon.

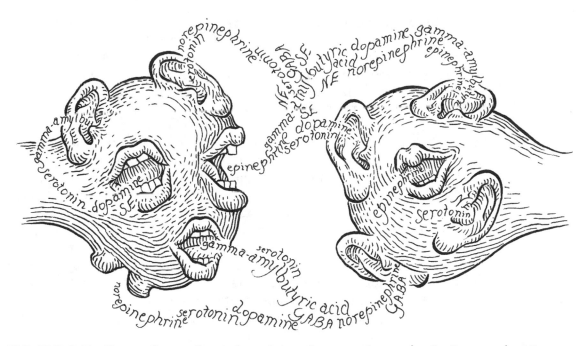

FIGURE 2-5   The synaptic space. The actual space between the presynaptic neuron (sending the message) and the postsynaptic neuron (receiving the message).

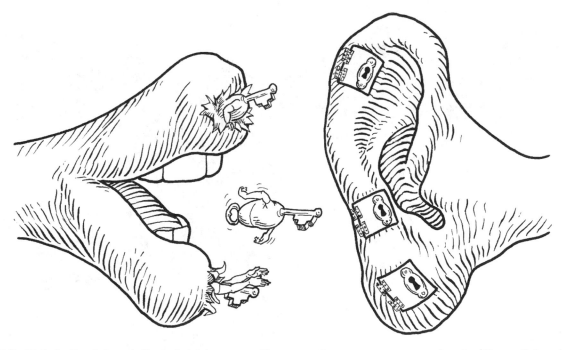

FIGURE 2-6   Schematic illustration of the synapse. The presynaptic neuron on the left is the "speaker," the one that sends the message; the postsynaptic neuron on the right is the "listener," the one receiving the message. The neurotransmitter molecules are the "words," or the chemical messengers.

Why is it that neurons don't touch? For the same reason that humans don't go through life touching each other at all times. If we did, we wouldn't be able to feed, eliminate waste or most important, communicate. (Try talking to somebody with your mouth touching the other person, with no space for words to flow between the two of you.) The space between neurons is filled with extracellular fluid, which is a sea in which nutrients flow to neurons and in which neurons excrete their waste, and thus is necessary for their survival. But that space is also present so that neurotransmitters can flow through it, permitting communication between neurons.

In order to better understand the process of neuronal communication, we can divide the process into four phases: the presynaptic, synaptic, postsynaptic, and postpostsynaptic phase.

In the presynaptic phase, a signal originates in the cell body and travels down the axon, much like electricity traveling down a wire, to the end of the axon (Figure 2-7). Receipt of the signal at the presynaptic space causes the vesicles containing neurotransmitters to migrate to the presynaptic membrane and release their content of neurotransmitters into the synaptic space. This takes us to the synaptic phase (Figure 2-8), during

FIGURE 2-7   The presynaptic phase. A signal traveling down the axon reaches the presynaptic area of the neuron. This causes the packages (or vesicles) containing neurotransmitters to migrate to the presynaptic membrane. There the vesicles fuse with the presynaptic membrane and release their content of neurotransmitters into the synaptic space.

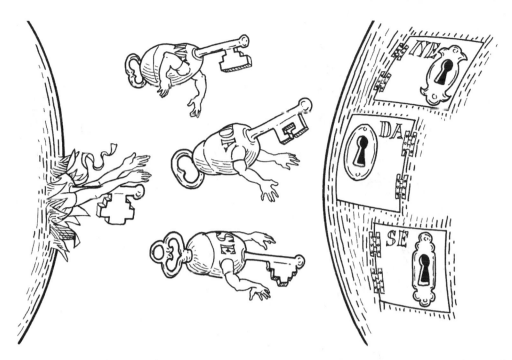

FIGURE 2-8   The synaptic phase. Neurotransmitter molecules released from the presynaptic neuron travel across the synaptic space to attach themselves to receptors.

which the molecules of neurotransmitters travel across the synaptic space and attach themselves to special sockets, called *receptors*, in the postsynaptic neuron. The attachment of the neurotransmitter to the receptor initiates the postsynaptic phase.

The receptor is specific for only a certain neurotransmitter. To illustrate this point, we can think of receptors as locks and neurotransmitters as keys. Just as only a specific key will fit a lock and open a door, so will a neurotransmitter with a very well-defined molecular structure fit into a specific receptor. Neurotransmitter molecules and receptors are also like soulmates, made only for each other. Each postsynaptic neuron has only a specific type of receptor, which can be activated by only specific neurotransmitters. In order for the neurotransmitter to stimulate a postsynaptic cell, it must find its receptor soulmate, and its soulmate must be available, unobstructed, ready to receive it. If a receptor is obstructed by another neurotransmitter molecule, it will be unable to attach to it (Figure 2-9). This is an important concept to understand because most drugs that act on the brain do so by posing as neurotransmitters and attaching themselves to receptors. By doing so, they can activate the cell or they can prevent the cell from being activated by the real neurotransmitter, which will find the receptor blocked by the drug.

Attachment of the neurotransmitter to the receptor will cause certain doors or channels located in the postsynaptic membrane to open, allowing certain ions to enter the cell from the extracellular fluid and from the cell into the extracellular fluid (Figure 2-10). This will cause a change in

FIGURE 2-9   A molecule of a "false" neurotransmitter attaches to a receptor and blocks it. When the real neurotransmitter comes along, it finds the receptor "taken" and is unable to attach to it.

the electrical charge of the neuron, which will aid in the process of neurotransmission.

What happens to the neurotransmitter once it has transmitted the signal to the postsynaptic cell? Think of two cells communicating with each other as two individuals conversing. The synapse is the physical space between the two people. Words that are spoken by the talking individual disappear from that space as soon as the other person hears them. If these words were to persist as an echo, communication would be confusing, if not impossible. Likewise, the neurotransmitter must disappear from the synapse after it has stimulated the receptor. In fact, as soon as the neurotransmitter has completed its rendezvous with the receptor, it detaches from it and immediately goes back into the synapse, where, if left to its own devices, it will attach itself to another free receptor (typical male behavior, according to a somewhat skeptic, twice-divorced female friend of mine). By this time, however, the synapse has become a dangerous territory for the neurotransmitter, since there are three forces committed to banishing it from there (Figure 2-11). The first force consists of enzymes, which are chemical substances in the synapse capable of destroying the neurotransmitter. The second force consists of the presynaptic cells, which, through a process called *reuptake*, "swallow" the neurotransmitter and either destroy it or recycle it to be used again (Figure 2-12). The third mechanisms consist of glial cells in the area, which will also ingest and destroy the neurotransmitter.

FIGURE 2-10   The postsynaptic phase. The attachment of the neurotransmitter molecular to its appointed receptor causes the doors or channels to open, permitting interchange of numerous molecules, including sodium and potassium, between the intracellular and extracellular spaces.

Another important issue in the communication between two cells is that of *neuronal feedback*, a process that is crucial to the normal operation of the brain. The brain is constantly obtaining feedback and adjusting its action in accordance with that feedback with every single one of its functions, whether language, movement, or emotion. At a neuronal level, feedback occurs as follows. Let's once more utilize the analogy of two people communicating. When one person speaks, the words not only reach the person listening, but they also reach the ears of the person talking, providing important feedback about the volume, content, and tone of that person's spoken words. This feedback loop allows the speaker to make

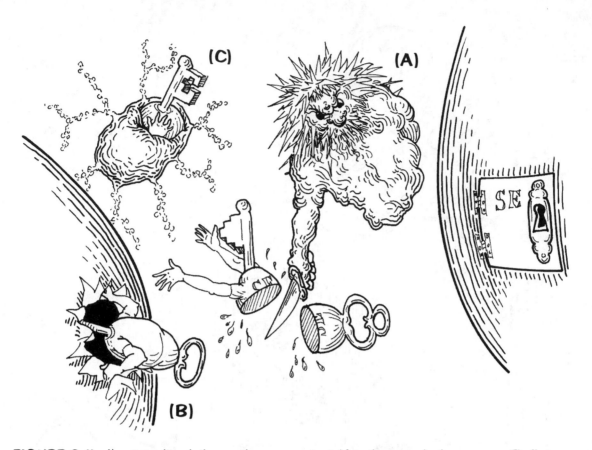

FIGURE 2-11   Neurotransmitters in the synaptic space are extracted from the synapse by three processes. The first consists of enzymes, which destroy the neurotransmitter molecule (A). The second consists of the reuptake of the neurotransmitters by the presynaptic neuron (B). The third consists of uptake of neurotransmitters by glial cells (C).

constant modifications in the messages she transmits. Similarly, via a number of mechanisms, the presynaptic neuron receives feedback about the message it sends. One of these is through means of *autoreceptors*, which are actually receptors located in the presynaptic neuron (Figure 2-13). These receptors function as a speaker's ears, "listening" to the chemical "words" emitted by the speaker. When a presynaptic neuron secretes neurotransmitter into the synapse, some of the neurotransmitter molecules stimulate these autoreceptors in the presynaptic neuron. These autoreceptors then inform the cell about the amount of neurotransmitter present in the synapse. This feedback mechanism is important to understand because, as we will see, certain drugs such as cocaine affect it. The second source of feedback is the postsynaptic cell itself, which sends a connection back to the presynaptic neuron, informing it that it has been stimulated (Figure 2-14).

Neurons are not, as previously thought, binary devices, able to transmit only an "on" or "off" message. Neurons can transmit an enormous number and variety of messages to other cells, defining the content of the message by varying, among other unknown variables, the type, quantity, and speed of release of a neurotransmitter. One neuron can "choose" to

FIGURE 2-12   Recycling of neurotransmitters by the presynaptic cell. After reuptake of the neurotransmitters by the synaptic neuron, the neurotransmitter molecule can either be "repackaged" (A) to be utilized again in the process of neurotransmission, or it can be broken down by enzymes (B) into raw material that will be used in the manufacture of new neurotransmitter molecules.

communicate with one other neuron or with a large number of other neurons. A neuron can utilize one neurotransmitter to communicate with one neuron while simultaneously utilizing another neurotransmitter to send a different message to another neuron (Figure 2-15).

What happens with the postsynaptic neuron after it receives a signal? First, the neuron must process the signal, which basically means deciding whether to send the signal to other neurons down the line. Although the reasoning it uses to come to a decision is not totally known, scientists have made much progress in understanding this matter in recent years. Different neurotransmitters send different signals to the postsynaptic neuron. Some, called *excitatory* neurotransmitters, encourage the neuron to transmit the

FIGURE 2-13   Auto feedback. Presynaptic neurons contain receptors for the same neurotransmitter that they release. Neurotransmitter molecules released by the presynaptic neuron can thus attach to these receptors, providing the presynaptic cell with information as to the number of neurotransmitters in the synapse.

signal to other neurons; others, the *inhibiting* transmitters, do exactly the opposite, instructing the neuron not to transmit information. Since a receiving neuron receives simultaneously inhibiting and excitatory signals from multiple sending neurons, part of the decision process involves summing up the excitatory and inhibiting signals. If the excitatory signals outnumber the inhibitory signals, the neuron will activate, or *depolarize*,

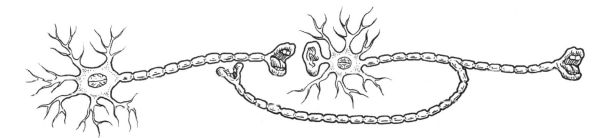

FIGURE 2-14 Auto feedback. A projection from the postsynaptic neuron is directed to the presynaptic neuron to provide feedback as to the state of communication.

producing the release of neurotransmitters as detailed above and sending the signal to other neurons. The matter, however, is not so simple. A number of other factors, some poorly understood, are involved in this information processing by neurons.

How many neurons does it take to fall in love? It is clear that certain activities require the participation, or *recruitment*, of a larger number of neurons than other activities. For example, a much greater number of neurons are involved in movement of the face and hands than are devoted to movement of the legs and feet. The reason is that although one neuron is responsible for communicating with a large number of muscle fibers of the feet, neurons involved in movement of the hands, a much finer and delicate movement, communicate with a much smaller number of muscles in the fingers. That is to say, the ratio of the number of neurons to number of muscle cells is much larger for the face and hands. The same holds true for sensation in the face and hands, compared with sensation in other areas of the body. This concept is illustrated by the homunculus.

The brain devotes a large proportion of neurons to activities such as language. Likewise, falling in love probably involves a very large number of neurons.

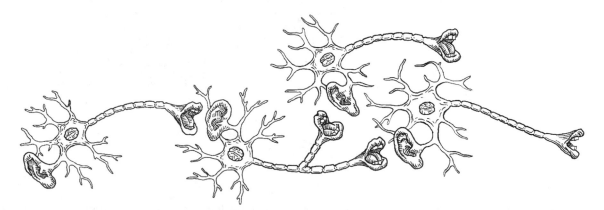

FIGURE 2-15 One neuron can receive information from and send information to several neurons simultaneously.

GLIAL CELLS

There are two types of glial cells. The first, called *astrocytes*, have a number of important functions (Figure 2-16). They provide physical support by forming a mesh in which neurons are situated, and they have a fundamental role in regulating the composition of the environment in which nerve cells reside. Astrocytes, and probably other glial cells, have been found to maintain the chemical equilibrium in the extracellular space.

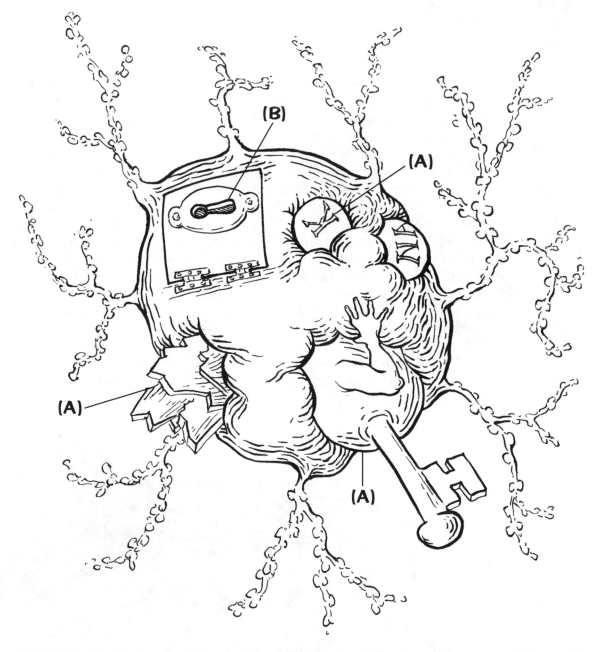

FIGURE 2-16   Functions of astrocytes. Besides providing physical support to neurons, astrocytes remove debris as well as excess neurotransmitters from the extracellular space (A). They also regulate the concentration of several ions and contain neurotransmitter receptors (B), suggesting that they also play a significant role in neurotransmission.

They also remove debris, such as dead cells resulting from injury, from the extracellular space. They act as scavengers by eliminating waste produced by neurons and other cells, and they facilitate the acquisition of necessary nutrients. The blood-brain barrier, which we will discuss in later sections and which allows only certain substances to pass from the bloodstream into the brain, is partially made up of glial cells, along with other types of cells. Astrocytes also regulate to a certain extent the communication between neurons by destroying neurotransmitter molecules in the extra cellular space. In recent years, receptors to neurotransmitter have also been found in the membrane of astrocytes, suggesting that they may play a greater role than previously thought in communication within neurons.

The second types of glial cell, called *oligodendrocytes* and *Schwann cells*, are responsible for preventing abnormal communication between neurons by means of an interesting mechanism. Oligodendrocytes are located in the central nervous system (the brain and spinal cord), and Schwann cells are located in the peripheral nervous system. These cells contain within themselves an insulating material called *myelin*. Oligodendrocytes and Schwann cells wrap themselves around the axons of neurons, much as a plastic insulating material is wrapped around the metal portion of a wire to prevent short-circuits with other wires (Figure 2-17). Unlike plastic wrapping, however, myelin sheaths, as they are called, are part of a "live wall." This live wall allows neurons to work close to each other without short-circuiting. Additionally, through an involved process, myelin allows for faster conduction of information throughout the axon. Oligodendrocytes wrap around multiple axons, Schwann cells insulate only one axon (Figure 2-18).

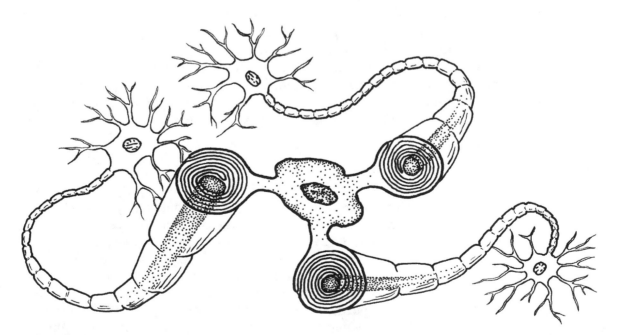

FIGURE 2-17   Oligodendrocytes wrap themselves around neurons (seen in cross-sections), aiding in the process of neurotransmission.

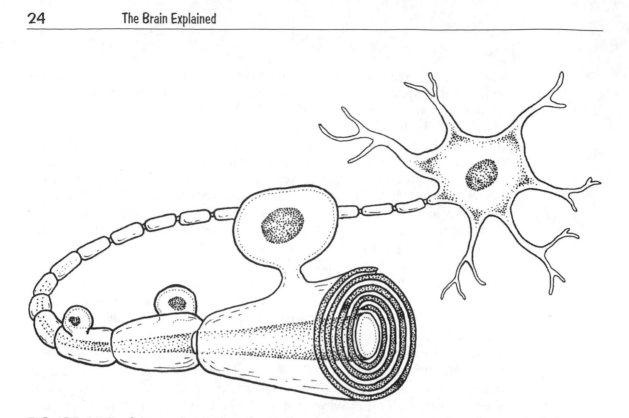

FIGURE 2-18   Schwann cells, which are present in the peripheral nervous system, wrap themselves around a single axon, unlike oligodendrocytes, which can wrap themselves around several axons simultaneously.

Signs of Malfunction

A number of conditions, too numerous to name in this manual, can affect and damage neurons. Since the main function of neurons is to process information and communicate with other neurons, injury to a neuron can in varying degrees affect its ability to do its job. Certainly, a dead neuron loses the ability to communicate altogether. A damaged neuron can lose its ability to communicate permanently or for a limited period of time. It may fail to communicate altogether or it may become hyperexcitable, which means that it will communicate in an erratic fashion, resulting in various neurological manifestations.

In recent years, the deficiency or excess of certain neurotransmitters has been implicated in a number of disorders of the brain. For example, a deficiency of dopamine has been identified as the culprit for Parkinson's disease. An excess of dopamine, along with a deficiency of GABA and acetylcholine, has been implicated in a fatal condition called Huntington's disease. A deficiency of acetylcholine has been found in patients with Alzheimer's disease. A number of psychiatric disorders, including depression, bipolar disorders, and schizophrenia, have been associated with alterations in the level of numerous neurotransmitters such as dopamine, serotonin, norepinephrine, GABA, and many others. An excess of norepinephrine and a deficiency in serotonin have been implicated in individuals committing acts of aggression.

However, the matter is not as simple as it seems. In rare cases, such as in Parkinson's and Alzheimer's, scientists have used sophisticated techniques to demonstrate altered levels of neurotransmitters in the brain. In other disorders such as depression and schizophrenia, scientists have assumed that there may be an alteration in the levels of neurotransmitters because drugs useful in the treatment of those disorders are known to affect neurotransmitter levels. In recent years, several lines of evidence have suggested that this assumption may be incorrect.

Rather than viewing neurological and psychiatric disease as an alteration in the levels of neurotransmitters, we should view such disease as an alteration in the communication between neurons. Since neurotransmitters are the chemical language utilized by neurons to communicate, their level may be affected secondarily to problems with communication. Alterations in the communications between neurons can occur at a number of levels:

1. At the presynaptic level, communication could be impaired for a number of reasons. Levels of neurotransmitters could decrease because the individual presynaptic neuron is not producing enough neurotransmitter, either because it lacks the necessary raw products (a rare situation) or because the machinery necessary for the manufacturing is damaged. The number of total presynaptic neurons could also decrease because of damage or death, thus decreasing the total number of neurotransmitters, as occurs in many diseases of the brain, such as Alzheimer's or Parkinson's. Or it may be that the presynaptic neuron is able to manufacture neurotransmitters normally, but the mechanism for its release from the cell to the synapse is impaired, as occurs in botulism.

2. At the synapse level, an increase or decrease in the number of enzymes may be responsible for breaking down neurotransmitters, as is seen with the use of many drugs. The number of neurotransmitters in the synapse may also increase because the presynaptic reuptake mechanism, which normally decreases neurotransmitter in the synapse, is not functioning properly. This occurs with the use of cocaine.

3. At the postsynaptic level, the number of receptors in individual neurons or the total number of postsynaptic neurons could increase or decrease. This is also seen with many diseases of the brain, such as Huntington's and Alzheimer's.

How can we voluntarily modify the amount and activity of neurotransmitter in the brain? There are several ways:

1. If we wanted to *increase* a particular neurotransmitter, we could ingest the *precursor*, the raw materials used by the neuron to manufacture a particular neurotransmitter. For example, choline, a substance commonly found in certain food products, is utilized by brain cells to produce acetylcholine. L-Dopa, a component of Dopamine, can also be given as a drug to Parkinson's patients. Ingesting the precursor will in

some instances result in an increase in the level of a neurotransmitter. This subject is discussed in more detail in the chapter on nutrition. Alternatively, we could stimulate the presynaptic cell to release a greater number of neurotransmitters. This is the mechanism by which electroconvulsive shock is believed to act in the treatment of depression. The electrical current stimulates certain neurons to release a number of neurotransmitters, including norepinephrine, which is believed to be affected in depression. We also could potentiate the action of a neurotransmitter on a postsynaptic cell via drugs such as benzodiazepines. (Valium is such a drug.) These agents principally have an effect on receptors to the neurotransmitter GABA. When benzodiazepines bind to a component of the GABA receptor, the effect of the binding of the actual neurotransmitter GABA to the receptor is magnified. In yet another alternative, we could increase the amount and activity of a neurotransmitter at the level of the synapse by agents that block the enzymes responsible for its breakdown. We could accomplish this using the drug physostigmine (see Figure 2-19), which blocks the synaptic destruction of acetylcholine (used to treat the common disorder Myasthenia gravis). A similar feat could be achieved by blocking the reuptake of a neurotransmitter by the presynaptic neuron. This will result in an increase in concentration of the neurotransmitter in the synapse. Many of the

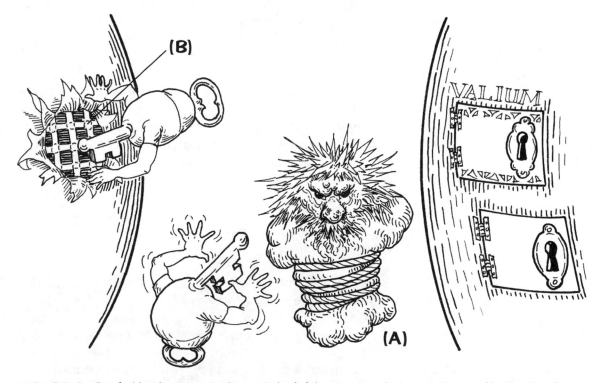

FIGURE 2-19   Activity of a neurotransmitter at the level of the synapse can be increased by several interventions. Certain drugs can act on enzymes that participate in the breakdown of the neurotransmitter molecules (A). Others can prevent the reuptake of the neurotransmitters by the presynaptic neuron (B), increasing the number of available neurotransmitters at the synaptic level.

newer antidepressants, such as Prozac, work by preventing the re-uptake of serotonin, which increases its level at the synapse. Cocaine and other drugs exert their influences in the brain via a similar mechanism. Finally, we could interfere with the breakdown of a neurotransmitter, which normally takes place after it has undergone reuptake from the synapse by the presynaptic cell. Selegeline, a drug used to treat Parkinson's disease, blocks the destruction of dopamine once it has undergone reuptake into the presynaptic neuron. This increases the availability of dopamine to be released by the presynaptic neuron.

2. If we wanted to *decrease* the activity of a neurotransmitter we could decrease the ingestion of the precursor. This rarely occurs, however. Alternatively, we could administer medications that block the manufacture of the neurotransmitter in the neuron, or we could use agents that block the release of the neurotransmitter into the synapse. This is how botulism toxin and black widow spider venom work, preventing the release of acetylcholine necessary for muscle contraction. As another alternative, we could use medications that block the receptor at the postsynaptic level so that when the neurotransmitter comes along, it will find the receptor blocked. This is how curare, a paralyzing agent used by Amazon jungle hunters, works. Muscle contraction results from the neuronal release of acetylcholine, which attaches itself to receptors in muscles and causes them to contract. Curare attaches itself and blocks the acetylcholine receptor, thus preventing the attachment of acetylcholine and leading to paralysis of all muscles, including those responsible for respiration.

The Concept of Excitotoxicity

In recent years, scientists have begun to understand that an excess of certain neurotransmitters within the synapse during particular times may be responsible for damage to neurons in a number of conditions, including strokes, head injury, and other disorders. Because this process occurs more frequently due to the excess of excitatory neurotransmitters, the process has come to be called *excitotoxicity*. This is an exciting discovery because it could potentially lead to improved treatment of these conditions.

The neurotransmitter most often implicated has been *glutamate*, an excitatory neurotransmitter widely distributed throughout the brain. During conditions such as strokes and traumatic brain injury, it appears that an excess of glutamate is released into the synapse by presynaptic neurons. The factors responsible for this excess of neurotransmitter release are not well understood, but the excess overrides the normal mechanisms responsible for removing glutamate from the synapse, such as reuptake by presynaptic neurons and uptake by glial cells. The large quantities of glutamate present in the synapses cause an excessive stimulation of postsynaptic neurons.

Glutamate is an interesting neurotransmitter. The binding of glutamate to a specific type of receptor, called the NMDA receptor, which is present in the postsynaptic cell, will cause certain doors (called *channels*) in the postsynaptic wall to open and allow calcium to flow into the cell. Under normal conditions, this calcium entry causes a number of beneficial changes in the postsynaptic cell. (We discuss those changes later under the topic of cellular learning.) However, excessive release of glutamate by presynaptic cells in conditions such as stroke and head injury results in an overestimulation of the postsynaptic neuron, resulting in opening of an excessive number of calcium channels. This in turn causes an excessive amount of calcium to enter the postsynaptic neuron (Figure 2-20). Excessive amounts of calcium are toxic to neurons, resulting in damage and even death.

This is not to say that all the damage to neurons that occurs during strokes and traumatic brain injuries is caused by excitotoxicity; many other factors contribute to damage. However, it appears that a significant proportion of neuronal injury and death occurs as a result of this mechanism.

Can this damage be prevented? In theory, it can. If damage is produced by an excessive amount of glutamate at the level of the synapse, blocking the postsynaptic receptors by other agents prevents the binding of glutamate to those receptors. That is to say, when the glutamate mole-

FIGURE 2-20   The process of excitotoxicity. Damage to the presynaptic neuron causes the excessive release of the neurotransmitter glutamate. This causes excessive activation of NMDA receptors, which will result in an excess of calcium entering the postsynaptic neuron. This in turn can cause damage or death to the postsynaptic neuron.

cule attempts to bind to the postsynaptic receptor, it will find it blocked by another molecule. This will prevent receptor stimulation by the gluta- mate, preventing the excessive influx of calcium into the postsynaptic cell.

In practice, unfortunately, this process is not as simple as it seems. The damage caused by excitotoxicity occurs at the time of injury or shortly thereafter; that is, at the time of onset of the stroke or the traumatic brain injury. Therefore, NMDA receptor blockers need to be given before or shortly after the injury in order for them to be effective. Indeed, animal studies have shown that administration of NMDA blockers before, at the time of, or shortly after injury results in much less neuronal injury than in situations where these agents are not administered at all.

Still, the development of newer, more effective NMDA receptor blockers and of systems for early administration of these agents show a lot of promise for reducing the amount of neuronal damage resulting from many neurological disorders.

Glial cells can also be the seat of a number of neurological diseases. Because of their supportive role to neurons, glial cells suffering diseases severely interfere with functions of the brain. One of the most dramatic disorders of oligodendrocytes is that of multiple sclerosis, which affects myelin. Because myelin is fundamental for the transmission of an impulse throughout an axon, any amount of damage to myelin will severely impede communication between neurons.

THE BIG PICTURE: STRUCTURE OF THE BRAIN

If you were to look at a brain in front of you, several characteristics would stand out:

1. The human brain is not particularly a pretty sight. It looks old and wrinkled, very much like a dried prune. However, this wrinkled appearance serves an extremely important function. You can demonstrate this function by holding a blank piece of standard letter paper in your hand. Since it measures 4 inches by 11 inches, its surface area is 44 inches. Now wrinkle and crumple that piece of paper as much as you can; you'll be able to place it inside your clenched hand. The surface area of the piece of paper is unchanged, but by wrinkling it as you did, you were able to fit it in a much smaller space than when it had its original shape. The same holds true for the brain. By being wrinkled as it is, it is able to maintain a huge surface area in spite of being able to fit inside of your skull, a relatively small space. Maintaining a large surface area is important because most brain cells are located on the surface of the brain.

2. The consistency of the brain is somewhere between that of Jell-O and a soft rubber ball. Its average weight is 1450 grams, or about 3

pounds, but interestingly, in adults it can range in weight from 1100 to 1700 grams. The weight of a person's brain has no relation to the person's body weight. In fact, obese individuals do not have overweight brains. The significance of this wide range in brain weight among individuals is unknown. On average, the brain is larger in males, but the brain/body weight ratio, which is a better indicator of brain development than is absolute weight, is greater in females. Differences in brain characteristics between men and women are discussed later in this manual.

3. The brain fits very well in a custom-built case made of bone (called the *cranial cavity*), which is located in your skull. Within the cranial cavity, the brain is surrounded on all sides by a clear fluid (called *cerebrospinal fluid*), which acts as a cushion, keeping the soft brain from touching the hard walls of the cavity at any time, even during normal movement. If not for this fluid, the brain would be constantly damaged from striking the walls of the cavity when you move your head.

4. As discussed earlier, all neurons in the brain are highly specialized to perform one task and to do it well. No neurons are general practitioners, able to do several things well. All neurons become specialists. Additionally, all neurons with similar specializations and tasks to perform gang up together and are localized in one particular area of the brain. Therefore, specific brain functions such as movement, vision, emotions, language, memory, reading, and control of body functions are each localized in a specific area of the brain. This fact has a number of advantages and disadvantages. Close physical proximity allows for easier communication among neurons of a functional type as well as more efficient operation. (As an analogy, imagine if all the employees involved in accounting or delivery of supplies were scattered in different areas in a manufacturing plant.) This agglomeration, however, results in greater vulnerability as far as the performance of a function is concerned. If a bomb were to fall in the area responsible for accounting in a plant, or if one of the employees in that department came in with a flu and infected all those in close proximity to him so that they could not work, the whole accounting function would be wiped out. Similarly, if a stroke involves even a small area of the brain, but that area happens to be the one responsible for language, a person's ability to communicate would be affected.

5. The brain consists of gray and white matter. That is, if we were to look at a cross-section of the brain, some parts appear gray and others white. This is because the gray matter consists of neuronal bodies, and the white matter consists of axons. In the architecture of the brain, the cell bodies of neurons with a common particular function are grouped together, as discussed. Macroscopically, this group looks like a gray area. The axons from those groups of neurons course together

in their way to communicate with other groups of neurons. These groups of axons appear to the naked eye to be white. The white appearance is due to myelin, discussed earlier. The surface of the brain is all gray matter; the areas underneath it are mostly white matter. However, intermingled with this white matter are pockets or islands of neuronal bodies, forming groups such as the thalamus, basal ganglia, hypothalamus, and others.

6. The brain consists of multiple areas; the following sections discuss the cerebrum, the thalamus, the basal ganglia, the brainstem, and the cerebellum. The spinal cord, although not technically part of the brain proper, is discussed because of its importance. Figures 2-21 to 2-26 illustrate different views of the brain as seen from several positions. The areas discussed in the following paragraphs can be identified in these illustrations.

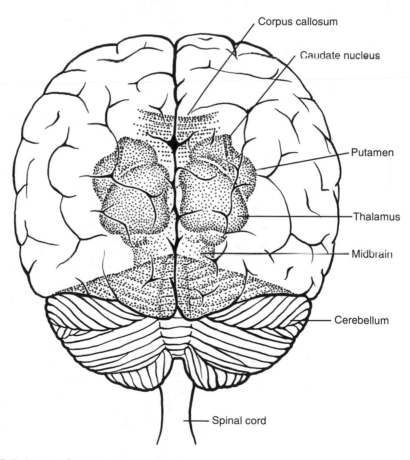

FIGURE 2-21   Brain viewed from the back.

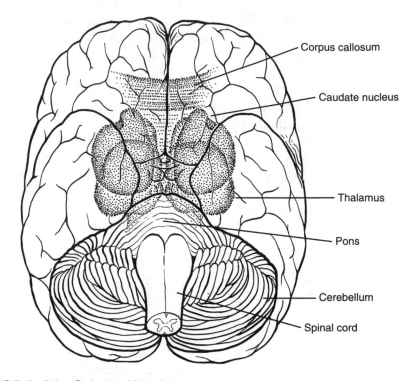

FIGURE 2-22   Brain viewed from the bottom.

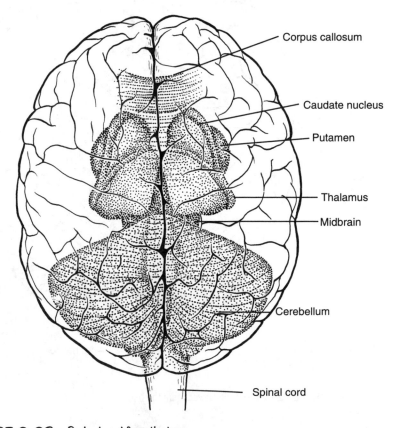

FIGURE 2-23   Brain viewed from the top.

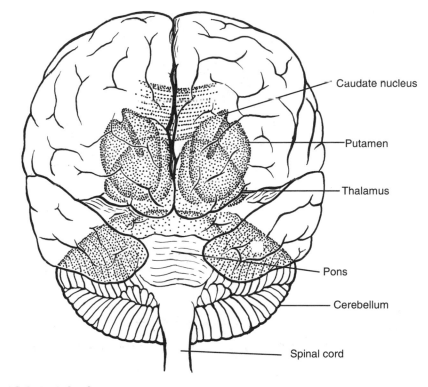

FIGURE 2-24 Brain viewed from the front.

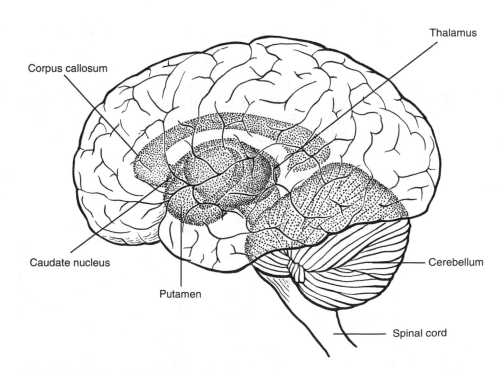

FIGURE 2-25 Brain viewed from the side.

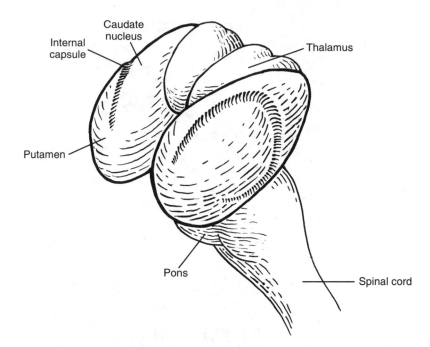

FIGURE 2-26   Diagram of the brainstem, thalamus and caudate nucleus.

The Cerebellum

The *cerebellum* has a number of functions, but one of its main purposes is to assure that all movements in your body are smooth and accurate. To illustrate this point, take a simple test. Sit down in a chair, put both of your palms on your knees, close your eyes, and slowly move your right index finger from your knee to the tip of your nose and then back to the knee.

    This seemingly simple movement is extraordinarily complex, involving the teamwork of billions of brain and muscle cells. Initially, your cerebrum ordered the muscles of your arm and hand to perform the movement, but the brain component responsible for coordinating all the muscle cells, making sure that some cells relax and others contract, that the hand moves neither too slow nor too fast so that you do not hit your nose, and that it moves in the right direction even though your eyes are closed, is the cerebellum. The cerebellum can be compared to an air traffic controller, making all the calculations and adjustments to the muscle cells so that your index finger lands correctly and at the right speed on the tip of your nose. Just like the air traffic controller, the cerebellum collects an incredibly complex amount of information and feedback, including the speed of movement, the position of your hand at each fraction of a second, the position of your nose, and any obstacles that may be present in the path to guide your finger in a smooth and exact journey ending on the tip of your nose. The cerebellum is also involved in maintaining your balance, monitoring the position of your body at all times so that when you walk, run, and play sports, all the muscles in your body work together to maintain your erect or desired position. If you consider the tremendous complexity of movement involved in running, talking, writing, dancing, playing a musical instrument, and painting, you can begin to develop appreciation for your own cerebellum.

In addition to its role in the coordination of movement, the cerebellum; appears to have a prominent role in motor and non-motor learning. *Motor learning* refers to the learning of movement sequences necessary to perform a certain motor task (for example, the learning of sequential movements necessary to ride a bicycle). *Non-motor learning* refers to the learning of activities not requiring the learning of movement sequences. The exact role of the cerebellum in this scheme is not well understood.

Additionally, the cerebellum appears to have a prominent role in cognition, including planning of daily activities, speed of information processing, memory, and other cognitive processes.

Signs of Malfunction.   Damage to the cerebellum can occur from strokes, tumors, multiple sclerosis, toxins (in particular mercury), and a number of other conditions. Additionally, the cerebellum is very sensitive to the effects of alcohol. Even small amounts of alcohol affect a person's capacity to perform smooth and accurate movements, and larger amounts seriously affect coordination and balance, a fact well known to policemen assessing people for drunk driving. Think of the effect of alcohol on the cerebellum as the effect of alcohol on an air traffic controller. You would not want a drunk traffic controller directing the landing of the plane you are flying on, just as you would not want a drunk cerebellum coordinating and directing all of the movements involved in walking, running, driving or even moving your index finger from your knee to the tip of your nose in front of a traffic cop.

Because speech involves the coordination of multiple muscles of the chest, mouth, throat, and tongue, cerebellar damage will also result in speech abnormalities, such as dysarthria, or slurred speech. Certain disorders in cognition, including the timing and planning of activities, among many others, have been described in patients with diseases of the cerebellum.

The Brainstem

The *brainstem* gets its name from the fact that it looks very much like the stem of a tree. If you envision your brain as a bunch of broccoli, the little leaves would be the neurons in the cerebrum, and the stem would be your brainstem. The brainstem contain two types of structures: command centers (or nuclei) and information highways.

First, the brainstem contains a two-way highway (Figure 2-27). On one side are axons transmitting information from the brain to all of the organs and muscles in the body. For example, if you decide to move your right leg, the signal or command originates in the cerebrum and travels down the brainstem to the spinal cord and finally to the muscles of the leg. On the other side are axons transmitting information in the opposite direction, that is, from the body to the brain. If you close your eyes and someone

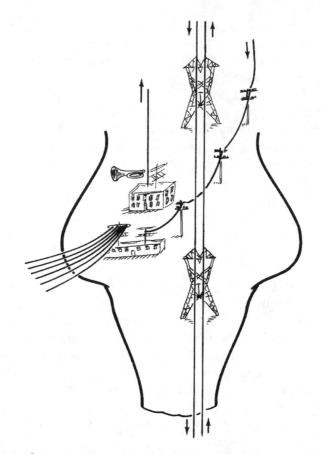

FIGURE 2-27   Schematic representation of the brainstem. The brainstem contains command posts (or nuclei) for the cranial nerves, centers responsible for consciousness and wakefulness and tracts conveying information from the brain to the spinal cord and vice versa.

puts a penny in your hand and asks you to identify what it is, information gathered by receptors in the skin flow from the hand to the spinal cord, up the brainstem to your hemispheres, which interpret the signals and identify the object as a penny.

Also on the brainstem are command posts, called *nuclei* (plural of *nucleus*), consisting of a group of neurons responsible for three types of actions. The first group of nuclei is involved with movement of the muscles of the eyes, mouth, face, throat, and neck. With respect to these nuclei, the brain operates in a sort of chain of command, where neurons in the cerebrum order nuclei in the brainstem to send the signal to muscle cells. If you voluntarily decide to close or move your eyes, smile, or stick out your tongue, the command originates in the hemisphere, where the neurons order the neurons in the nucleus of your brainstem to do the job. Some of the nuclei are also responsible for sensation in areas in the head, including the mouth and face.

The second group of nuclei consists of command posts for control of most of the body's organs, including the respiratory, cardiac, and gastrointestinal systems. For example, this group contains the "respiratory center" that operates automatically without the need for conscious control. That means that even though you do have some control over how fast or slow you breathe, the brainstem has the ultimate control. If you were to hold your breath, the brainstem would override you and force you to breathe after a certain period of time.

Finally, the brainstem also contains groups of neurons (or nuclei) responsible for regulating consciousness and the sleep/wake cycle. Some nuclei are responsible for maintaining consciousness and others for generating a stage of sleep called REM sleep, which, as we will see later, is the stage of sleep during which dreaming takes place. During this stage of sleep, the brainstem sends electrical discharges to numerous areas of the brain, a process theorized by some to be the cause of dreaming.

Signs of Malfunction.   Depending on where in the brainstem the damage is located, a number of problems can occur. First, interruption of the pathways transmitting information from the cerebrum to the rest of the body results in a person becoming paralyzed, because the signals originating in the cerebrum, which command the muscles to move, cannot reach the particular muscles. Similarly, damage to the pathways carrying information from the body to the brain results in a loss of sensation or feeling in the body.

Damage to the command centers for movement of the eyes, face, and mouth results in the inability to move these body parts. Damage to the nuclei responsible for consciousness results in coma or other disorders of consciousness. Finally, damage to centers responsible for control of some of the body's organs, such as the respiratory center, could result in death, such as resulting from paralysis of respiration.

The Thalamus

The *thalamus*, the brain's information censor and gatekeeper, is an extremely complex structure of the brain which has several functions. The first consists in the maintenance of arousal or wakefulness, a topic which we discuss in more detail in the chapter on consciousness. The second role of the thalamus is to act as a relay station, receiving information from all of the sensory organs and then sending the information on to the cerebral cortex. The reason information from the sensory organs makes a stop in the thalamus in its way to the cortex as opposed to proceeding directly to the cortex is not entirely clear. The thalamus appears to have an important role in the selection, ordering, and organization of the information from the sensory organs before it reaches the cortex. It is thus the first "processing station" for information stemming from the outside world and proceeding to the cortex. Additionally, the thalamus has an important role in the coordination of movement. The thalamus also has an important role in *autonomic functions*, that is, the control of the brain over functions of the body's organs. Finally, the thalamus appears to have an important, although poorly understood, role in cognition, especially memory.

Signs of Malfunction.   Thalamic lesions result in a number of complex clinical conditions. Because sensory pathways from the senses to the cortex are interrupted, sensory loss is one of the main manifestations. Motor abnormalities are frequent because of the role of the thalamus in movement. Problems in consciousness can also occur, as we discuss in other sections.

The Basal Ganglia

The *basal ganglia* include a group of nuclei such as the putamen, globus pallidus, caudate nucleus, substantia nigra, and subthalamic nucleus. The functions of the basal ganglia are not entirely understood, but they appear to have a prominent role in the *initiation* and coordination of simple and complex movement and the maintenance of muscle tone. There is also increasing evidence that some portions of the basal ganglia have a fundamental role in cognition. Much of what is known about the function of the basal ganglia stems from evaluating the symptoms displayed by patients with diseases of the basal ganglia.

Signs of Malfunction.   Damage to the basal ganglia can result in a number of disorders that have a number of clinical manifestations in common, including cognitive and behavioral problems as well as disorders in movement. Furthermore, damage to specific basal ganglia nuclei produce particular diseases, each with distinct characteristics and clinical features. Parkinson's disease, for example, results from damage to the substantia nigra and results in tremor and bradykinesia (slowness of movement), among other features. On the other hand, Huntington's disease results from damage to the caudate nucleus and results in behavioral problems, dementia, and an excess of abnormal movements (chorea, which are abrupt movements of the limbs and facial muscles), among a number of other signs and symptoms. Wilson's disease, which results from the accumulation of copper in the basal ganglia, also results in dementia and behavioral and movement abnormalities. Many of the diseases involving the basal ganglia, such as Huntington and Wilson's, have a strong and well-studied genetic basis. By comparison, the underlying cause for Parkinson's disease is not well known. Other diseases of the basal ganglia, such as hemiballismus, which results in violent swinging of the arms or legs, is caused from acquired injury to the subthalamic nucleus resulting from disorders such as strokes.
There is a close link between specific basal ganglia and the neurotransmitters that they utilize to communicate with other cells. This association can be advantageously used in the treatment of these disorders. For example, the substantia nigra utilizes dopamine. Parkinson's disease, which we learned results from damage to the substantia nigra, results in a deficit of dopamine in the brain. This deficit can be corrected, to a limited degree, with the ingestion of raw materials that brain cells will turn into dopamine. Huntington's disease causes an alteration in the level of GABA and acetylcholine within the basal ganglia, although other neurotransmitters are involved. Unfortunately, there is little in the way of treatment for this disease.

The Cerebrum

The *cerebrum* is the brain of the brain. It contains two hemispheres, which are essentially mirror images of each other, although minor differences exist between them, as we discuss later. Each hemisphere is divided into five areas, each with a specific function: the frontal, parietal, temporal, and occipital lobes and the insula (Figure 2-28).

Before proceeding with discussion of the function of individual areas within the cerebrum, it is important to understand the following: The brain handles information in a sort of hierarchical fashion, where information is processed from the simple to the complex. In order to do this, it contains *primary*, *secondary*, and *tertiary* areas for processing visual, auditory, and sensory information, as well as for motor output. For example, in the visual system, information reaching the eyes in the form of light beams is transduced into electrical impulses that reach the primary area for visual information. The primary area thus receives raw data, consisting of certain shapes, which it transmits to the secondary visual area, which interprets this data as corresponding to the shape of a face. This data is then sent to the tertiary area, which further processes the data and identifies the face, not as just any face, but belonging to a person you know. Similarly, the primary auditory area receives sound waves from the ears, which it sends to the secondary area, which interprets this sound as words, which are then sent to

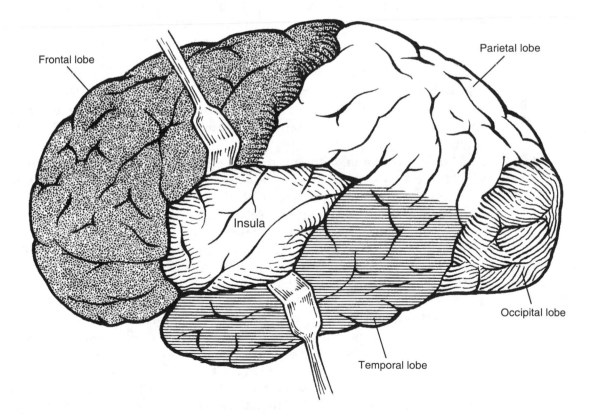

FIGURE 2-28   Side (or lateral) view of the brain showing the five lobes. The temporal and parietal lobes are being moved to expose the insula.

the tertiary area, which makes sense of the words. These primary, secondary, and tertiary areas are each specific for one type of information, in this case visual and auditory, but data from the tertiary areas, which has already been highly processed, is sent further along to *multimodal association areas*, which process information from combined visual, auditory, and sensory sources. These areas integrate the shape of a face with the sound of a voice to identify a specific person, for example.

The important concept to remember is that primary areas receive information directly from the outside world by means of the eyes, ears, and touch sensors. Secondary and tertiary areas have no direct contact with the outside universe, since they receive information only from primary and secondary brain areas, respectively.

In the case of movement, secondary and tertiary motor areas are responsible for complex motions that involve a large number of individual muscles, such as playing a guitar. These secondary and tertiary areas send instructions to the primary areas, which are responsible for movement of individual muscles.

Lobes of the Cerebrum.   The *frontal lobes* of the cerebrum have a number of functions. First, they are the initiators and the command post for most movement. If you walk, run, drive, or play a musical instrument, most signals to the muscles involved in these activities are initiated in the frontal lobes. Second, the *left* frontal lobe is responsible for the motor movement involved in language. Language has two components. The first is output, that is, the action of sending a message from yourself to others. The second is input, which refers to the interpretation of messages that others send you. The left frontal lobe is responsible for the output component. It is in charge of initiating and directing movement of the muscles in your mouth and your tongue when you speak, of your hand when your write, and of your whole body when you transmit information through body language.

Third, the frontal lobes are responsible for determining your personality, the way you are, the way you react to things that happen to you from minute to minute. *The frontal lobes are the black box that stands between a call to action (CTA) and a response.* Your brain is constantly being subjected to situations that require it to act. These situations, which we call CTA, can originate from within or outside your body. Hunger and thirst, the need to solve a problem, the way we react to being insulted or attacked, all are situations to which your frontal lobes must appropriately react, often within fractions of a second. In order to do so appropriately, the frontal lobes must go through a series of steps and make a number of decisions. They must search their memory stores to find whether similar situations were encountered in the past and how they reacted to them. They must consider all circumstances surrounding that CTA to decide whether to respond immediately or delay the response to a more appropriate time. They must consider a large number of potential responses, foresee the short- and long-term consequences of each, and decide on the most suitable one. Once they have decided on a strategy, they must implement it. They must modify the strategy if it is not successful or if a change in the circumstance surrounding the CTA mandates changing the strategy.

Fourth, they are responsible for drive, that mental energy that impels all psychological and physical activity.

Signs of Malfunction.   The frontal lobes can be damaged by strokes, brain tumors, trauma to the head, and certain dementia such as Alzheimer's disease. Depending on where in the frontal lobes the lesion is located, a number of clinical syndromes can occur.

First, damage to areas responsible for the initiation of movement interferes with a person's ability to move the opposite side of his or her face, arm and/or leg. Second, damage to the region responsible for speech output in the left frontal lobe results in a person's inability to speak, to varying degrees. The affected individual would be able to understand what was said to him, but would be unable to initiate or respond to speech. To all practical purposes, the person would become mute. Frequently, an affected individual would also be unable to write. A person with damage to the right frontal lobe would retain his ability to speak, but his speech would be monotonous, devoid of affective or emotional expression. There would be no difference in his speech whether he was afraid, angry, anxious, or happy.

A number of psychological and behavioral problems can also occur. Problems with drive or mental energy are common. Patients and their families complain that the affected individual frequently seems to lose the energy and interest to perform activities he or she previously did well and with relish. Loss of curiosity is frequently reported. Patients often tell me that they don't feel like doing anything, frequently neglecting their jobs and families. A previously highly dedicated mother of four who suffered frontal lobe injury from a motor vehicle accident was described by her husband as becoming excessively "lazy," neglecting him and their children. A formerly severely aggressive individual who underwent a frontal lobotomy to control aggression became calm, sitting around the hospital all day. When I asked him about his prior violent history, he stated that he had occasional thoughts of killing people, but that he didn't have the will or energy to do it any longer.

Other individuals with frontal lobe injuries become uninhibited, impulsive, frequently described by family members as "childlike." These people frequently get into trouble by responding to situations in an inappropriate fashion, failing to consider or foresee the consequences of their responses. A previously happily married patient with frontal lobe lesions from a motorcycle accident became exceedingly inappropriate (or extremely honest, as described by his wife) in what he said. For example, he would crudely complement female strangers on their physical attributes, even when his wife was present. Individuals with normal frontal lobe functions may nurse the same thoughts but will restrain themselves from voicing them at inappropriate times. Another previously placid factory worker of small stature who was injured in an industrial accident would constantly become involved in fights on being called "Shorty," even when his aggressor was taller and stronger than him. Failing to consider the consequences of his action, he would often be beaten up. A former conservative executive with frontal lobe damage got into the habit of telling inappropriate sexually implicit jokes in board meetings, to the dismay of his colleagues.

Patients with frontal lobe damage frequently have difficulty in carrying out tasks that require complicated planning and organization. For example, a supervisor in a school cafeteria lost the ability to plan menus and schedules after a frontal injury. Other patients lose the ability to change details in a pre-established plan when the need arises. A bridge engineer could plan the building of a bridge to the smallest detail after damage to his frontal lobes, but once his project was in the building stage, he had great difficulty in adjusting his plan to unforeseen circumstances, such as the temporary shortage of a building material or an unexpected change in the weather.

The Parietal Lobes.   The *parietal lobes* are responsible for processing all types of sensory information, including touch, pain, and the identification of objects through tactile information. Additionally, this area of the brain has a prominent role in the processing and understanding of language. Just as the frontal lobes are responsible for language output, the parietal lobes, together with the temporal lobes, are responsible for language input.

Lesions in the parietal lobes result in loss of sensation in the opposite side of the body. A person so affected will be unable to feel touch, temperature, and pain and will not be able to identify objects or people by touching them alone. Additionally, he or she could lose the capacity to understand language spoken by others. As with lesions in the temporal lobe, a person with parietal lobe lesions could retain the ability to talk but be unable to understand what others say to him or her or even what he himself says.

The Temporal Lobes.   The *temporal lobes* have a number of functions, including processing auditory information and, in the case of the left side, interpreting the meaning of language. They also have a prominent role in learning and memory and in modulation of emotions.

Damage to the temporal lobes can result in a number of problems. Disorders of learning and memory can occur and are discussed in more detail in subsequent chapters. Problems with the interpretation of language, denominated *receptive aphasia*, are common after damage to the left temporal area. Patients so affected are able to speak relatively well, since the area responsible for speech output in the frontal lobes is normal, but they are unable to understand spoken language, even their own. Written language is often not affected. Damage to the temporal lobes also results in problems with memory and in an inability to learn new information.

Emotional disturbances, including anger and rage attacks, have been associated with seizures involving the temporal lobes or nearby areas. Other symptoms found in patients with temporal lobe epilepsy include episodes of fear, anxiety, dèja vú feelings, and panic attacks. As we discuss in the chapter on the brain and aggression, the temporal lobes and surrounding areas have been implicated in the genesis of aggression and violence.

The Occipital Lobes.   The *occipital lobes* are responsible for processing visual information. The process of vision is very complex. As everywhere else in the brain, cells in the occipital area are highly specialized. Some cells are activated only by information about vertical lines, others by horizontal lines, and yet others to lines of a certain length. Still other cells respond only to certain colors or specific shapes. Some cells respond only to motion of various velocities. When information arrives from the eyes, each of these specialized cells contributes its bit of information to arrive at a mental image. Additionally, information carried from the eyes to the brain is processed in a hierarchical manner, where a first line of cells process simple visual information such as contrast and carry this information to a second layer of cells, which process shapes and then send this information to yet another layer, which interprets the shapes. Thus, each succeeding layer of cells is able to contribute additional information to the mental image until its meaning is determined.

Each occipital lobe processes information about half of the visual field. If you look directly in front of you and draw an imaginary vertical line at the level of your nose, you can divide the field of your vision into a right and left side. The left occipital lobe "sees" the right side of the field and the right lobe "sees" the left side. There are ample connections between both lobes so that information about each side is carried back and forth.

A number of syndromes can occur from damage to the occipital lobes. Total bilateral destruction, such as occurs after certain strokes, results in cortical blindness, where an individual cannot see, not due to anything wrong with his eyes, but due to inability of the brain to process visual information. Damage to one occipital lobe will result in blindness in the opposite visual field.

Other disorders of *visual recognition*, called *agnosias*, can also occur. Some patients lose the ability to recognize colors, faces, or common objects. Other individuals become unable to recognize certain specific categories of objects, such as fruits, tools, or animals. Still others lose the ability to detect depth or movement. A rare condition resulting from damage to certain parts of the occipital lobe is called Anton's syndrome, in which an individual is blind but denies being so.

BRAIN CONNECTIVITY

The brain can be compared to an infinitely sophisticated manufacturing plant that contains thousands of sections, each specialized in the performance of a particular function. For the successful operation of the plant, extensive and ongoing communication within sections is of the utmost importance. Thus, the section of the plant responsible for taking in orders must be able to communicate with the section manufacturing the product, which must communicate with the section providing supplies, and so on. A disruption in communication would result in a breakdown in the overall operation of the plant. Some sections may remain operational, but their work in isolation would be meaningless.

Similarly, virtually all areas of the brain extensively communicate with other areas, and this communication is the key to successful brain operation. Thus, the area responsible for speech input communicates with that responsible for speech output, the one for reading with that for writing, the area responsible for reception of visual information with that in charge of interpreting that information, and so on. As can be expected, any disruption in this extremely sophisticated communication system will seriously affect overall functioning of the brain.

Special mention must be made of the *corpus callosum*, which consists of a large group of axons connecting the brain's right and left hemispheres. Virtually all areas of the brain in one hemisphere are connected with other areas in the opposite hemisphere.

Disconnection syndromes are clinical conditions resulting from damage to the connections between areas of the brain. These syndromes can be caused by a number of lesions, including strokes, tumors, hemorrhages, and trauma. Disconnection syndromes can result in a number of clinical problems. Destruction of the fibers connecting both hemispheres results in an unusual syndromes in which each hemisphere functions in isolation from the other hemisphere. The popular saying, "The right hand does not know what the left hand is doing" is an excellent description for this condition. One of my patients displaying such a syndrome was unable to make both her hands work in unison to perform a task. For example, with her right hand she would stroke her pet cat while her left hand tried to drive the confused animal away. Similarly, she could read out loud but was unable to understand what she was writing. The connections between the reading areas in the right brain and the reading interpretation areas in the left brain were absent. A similarly affected carpenter could not make one hand hold a nail while the other hand used a hammer. Each hand would work in isolation, making him unable to come up with a finished product.

Disconnection between the areas responsible for receiving and understanding speech and the areas in charge of speech output is a common condition. The affected patient understands what he hears and is able to talk but is unable to repeat sentences or hold a meaningful conversation. There is little meaningful correlation between what he hears and what he says. Disconnection between areas responsible for vision and memory result in a person failing to recognize faces when he sees them, but that person is able to recognize the voices corresponding to those faces.

Differences in the Functions of the Right and Left Hemispheres

Although the brain's two hemispheres are almost mirror images of each other, there are some important differences in the functions that each performs. For example, speech is located in the left hemisphere in virtually all right-handed individuals and in most left-handed people. In some unusual cases, speech is localized in both sides, so damage to either will not affect speech. Likewise, intellectual and rational thinking occur on the left side.

The right hemisphere has an important function in the interpretation and expression of emotions. Thus, individuals with damage to the right side of the brain have prominent difficulty in identifying emotion contained in facial expressions. They fail to detect displays of emotions such as happiness, anger, or fear in other people's faces, a feat that can be easily accomplished even by babies of a few months of age. Interestingly, some investigators have suggested that representations of typical emotional facial expressions are encoded in the right side of the brain from birth. When we look at a face, we compare its features to these prototypes in our brain to elucidate its emotional expression. This explains why babies can identify the emotion expressed by their mothers without the need to "learn" the facial features associated with various emotions. Damage to the right hemisphere could destroy these facial emotional prototypes and leave an individual without the frame of reference to which to compare faces seen from day to day.

The right side of the brain is not only responsible for the *interpretation* of facial expressions in others but also for the *display* of emotions through facial expressions. Studies have shown that in normal individuals, the left side of the face, which is controlled by the right brain, is better at expressing emotions than the right side of the face, which is controlled by the left brain. Also, individuals with right hemispheric damage not only have difficulty in interpreting the emotions expressed in the facial expressions of others, but they themselves frequently have difficulty in expressing emotions through facial expressions.

The right hemisphere is also important in elucidating the emotional tone in everyday language. When we speak, we use two components to our words to convey a message. The first is the actual meaning of the words, and the other is the process of *prosody*, which refers to the changes in pitch, amplitude, tempo, and rhythm (the musical undertone to our language) in which we speak those words. In other words, the message another person receives depends not only on *what* we say, but also on *how* we say it. Prosody is used to convey an emotional message in addition to the meaning of the words. For example, if I say, "I'm going to the supermarket," I can use prosody to make my words sound angry, or casual, or happy. The right hemisphere is necessary for the correct interpretation of this emotional prosody. In an experiment in which normal individuals were asked to identify the mood of a recorded speaker, they were able to do so much better if the recording was broadcast to the left ear, which conveys information to the right brain, than if the same recording was played to the right ear, which conveys information to the left brain.

Individuals with damage to the right brain are not only unable to correctly identify the emotional tone expressed by others, but they also have difficulty using prosody to convey emotions. Thus, they frequently need to rely more on the meaning of words rather than on the tone in which the words are spoken. Interestingly, individuals who sustain damage to the left hemisphere (which as we have discussed is responsible for language) but have an intact right brain are much better at understanding and speaking emotional than non-emotional words, presumably because those words are generated and interpreted by the right hemisphere.

Recognition of complex, nonverbal images, such as that of faces or other three-dimensional figures, is performed by the right side of the brain. This side is also more adept at intuitive and emotional thinking. The processing of music is also lateralized to the right side.

Differences in Brain Characteristics Among Sexes

As discussed above, the average brain size is larger in males, but the brain/body weight ratio is greater in females. But perhaps one of the most fascinating recent discoveries in this subject is that *cerebral specialization*, which refers to the localization of a specific function to a particular area of the brain, occurs earlier and is more complete in males than in females. Thus, language becomes localized to the left side sooner in boys than in girls, so that damage to the left side is more likely to affect language in male children. The brains of girls seem to retain the capacity to respond to left hemispheric damage longer by transferring language to the right side (termed *brain plasticity*, or the ability of the brain to retain the capacity to change specialization depending on demands imposed on it). Right or left handedness, that is, the predominance of one hand in performing fine movements such as writing, also occurs earlier and more completely in boys. Therefore, girls are more likely to become able to use the opposite hand if the dominant one is damaged.

In adult patients, this increased plasticity of the female brain is less evident but still present to some degree. In males, there is a strong association between side of the damage and the function affected. Thus, left hemispheric strokes are more likely to affect language in males, while females with similar lesions may have less involvement of language functions.

The Spinal Cord

The spinal cord is a long tubular structure that is the downward continuation of the brainstem. It provides the link between the brain and areas of the body below the neck. Like the brain stem, the spinal cord is also in part an information highway, carrying fibers that relay information from the brain to the rest of the body and fibers coursing in the opposite direction—that is, from the body toward the brain.

The first category of fiber, from the brain to the rest of the body, consists of two groups. The first is the fiber that relays commands from the brain to all muscles of the body below the neck, thus permitting movement and regulating muscle tone. The second category is the fiber that carries information from the brain to all the organs of the body, as we discuss in the section on the autonomic nervous system.

A *tract* within the spinal cord consists of a bundle of axons with a common purpose. An example of a tract is the corticospinal tract, which transmits impulses from the brain to the body and is responsible for voluntary movement (Figure 2-29). The cell bodies of those axons are located in the brain, specifically in the areas in charge of volitional movement (the frontal motor cortex). The axons of those cell bodies travel via the corticospinal tract in the brain. Immediately below the brainstem, they cross over to the opposite side of the spinal cord until they reach the approximate area of the body containing the muscle to be moved. Therefore, fibers originating in the left side of the body cross over and travel on the right side of the spinal cord. The reason for

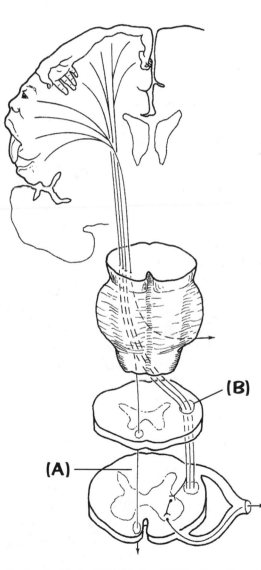

FIGURE 2-29   Descending tracts of the spinal cord. Pictured are the anterior (A) and lateral (B) spinothalamic tracts, carrying fibers from the cortex to corresponding muscle groups in the body. The motor homonculus is pictured.

this crossover is not fully understood, but the net effect is that the left side of the brain moves muscles of the right side of the body, and vice versa.

An interesting point is that the fibers of the corticospinal tract do not leave the spinal cord themselves to stimulate the muscle. Instead, they synapse with an intermediary neuron, called the *motor neuron*, which sends its axon out of the spinal cord and to the muscle. Therefore, at least two neurons are involved in movement, the first in the motor cortex, which sends its axon within the spinal cord to connect with the second neuron, the motor neuron, which sends its axon to connect and stimulate the particular muscle.

The axons from the motor neurons leave the spinal cord on their way to the muscles at periodic levels in bundles called *roots*. After emerging from the spinal cord, they merge with axons carrying information in the opposite direction, that is, from the body to the spinal cord and from there to the brain. The combined incoming and outgoing fibers comprise a nerve, which are literally the wires carrying information from and to the spinal cord.

The second category of fiber, carrying information from the body to the brain, belongs to several groups. First, there are those fibers carrying sensory information from receptors in the skin below the neck to the brain, conveying sensations of touch, pain, and temperature. Second, there are fibers carrying a specific type of sensory information called *propioception*, which consists of information from the skin, muscles, joints, and so on that provides details to the brain about the position of every part of the body at any one time. Third, there are those fibers carrying information from some of the body's organs, which we discuss in more detail when we explore the autonomic nervous system.

An example ascending tract is the spinothalamic tract, which transmits sensations of pain, temperature, and light touch from the body to the brain. This sensation is captured by *sensory receptors*, which are distributed throughout the skin, joints, and other areas of the body. Sensory receptors transduce a specific type of information, such as touch or temperature, into electrical impulses. These impulses are carried by nerves to the spinal cord, from there to the thalamus, and then on to the cortex. As with the corticospinal tract, axons transmitting information from one side of the body enter the spinal cord on the same side and almost immediately cross over to the other side, where they begin their ascent toward the brain (Figure 2-30). There are several neurons involved in this transmission. The first has its cell body outside of the spinal cord, the second within the spinal cord, the third in the thalamus, and then from there to neurons of the cortex. The fact that several neurons are involved indicates that information is processed in some way by each of them before that information reaches the cortex. If a fly lands on your arm (light touch), a receptor in your skin changes the sensation of touch into electrical impulses, transmitted by nerves to the spinal cord, where other neurons capture that information and carry it to the thalamus and from there to the cortex. This all happens within a fraction of a second.

Another important spinal ascending tract is made of two components, which make up what is called the Dorsal Column-Medial Lemniscal Sys-

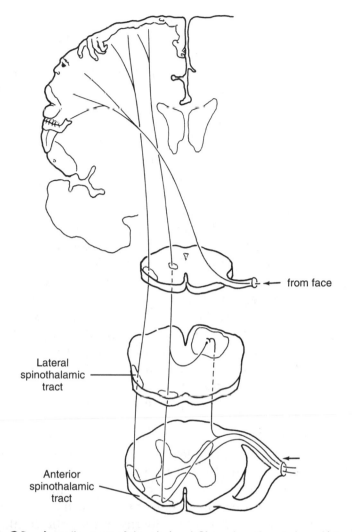

from face

Lateral
spinothalamic
tract

Anterior
spinothalamic
tract

FIGURE 2-30 Ascending tracts of the spinal cord. Pictured are the anterior and lateral spinothalamic tracts as well as the posterior columns.

tem. It is comprised of the fasciculus gracilus and the fasciculus cuneatus. These are tracts that transmit proprioception (awareness of the position of a body part within space), two-point discrimination (the ability to differentiate between one and two points close in space), and other touch and sensory modalities. The axons carrying this information enter the spinal cord on the same side as the information, ascend the spinal cord, and cross over to the other side higher up in the brainstem, on their way to the thalamus and then the cortex. As with the spinothalamic tract, several intermediary neurons play a role in this transmission.

These crossovers of sensory tract in the spinal cord and the brainstem signify that sensory information from the right side of the body is carried to the left side of the brain, and vice versa.

The spinal cord is not solely an information carrier. It also performs certain activities autonomously, without participation of the brain. For example, most reflexes, such as the knee jerk, are processed at the level of the spinal cord without input from the brain. This autonomous function of the spinal cord allows you to pull your hand away from a hot flame even before you have experienced the conscious feeling of being burned. The way this works is as follows: Pain and temperature receptors in your hand send impulses from your hand to the spinal cord, relaying the message that your hand is in the fire. The spinal cord sends impulses to muscles in your hand and arm with instructions to quickly withdraw your hand while simultaneously sending information to the brain informing it about the situation. The cir-cuit hand–spinal cord–hand is faster than the circuit hand–spinal cord–brain–spinal cord–hand, allowing for a faster withdrawal. Thus, the withdrawal movement was processed at the spinal cord level, saving time and preventing you from getting injured. Emerging scientific information suggests that other complex motor activities, such as gait, are at least in part coordinated at a spinal cord level, although clearly the brain plays a major role.

At regular intervals, nerves taking information from the brain to areas of the body and nerves bringing information from the body to the brain leave and enter the spinal cord through *roots*. Each root carries to and from the brain information about a specific area of the body.

Just as the brain is encased in a fortress made up of bone, the skull, so is the spinal cord encased in a bone fortress formed by a series of structures called the *vertebrae*. In a similar fashion as the brain, the spinal cord is surrounded by cerebrospinal fluid, which acts as a cushion against trauma.

Signs of Malfunction.   Damage to the spinal cord can have drastic consequences. Damage at any one level interrupts the flow of information from the spinal cord to the brain and from the brain to the spinal cord. Since conscious perception of sensory perception takes place at the brain, as we discuss in subsequent chapters, damage will result in inability to have sensation in the area of the body below the lesion. The command for voluntary movement of the body is initiated in the brain and carried to the muscles of the body by means of the spinal cord, so a spinal cord lesion results in loss of movement below the lesion. Additionally, since information about and to various organs of the body is carried in part by the spinal cord, a lesion disconnects, in part, the organs from the brain. Unfortunately, damage to the spinal cord can result from a number of disorders, including trauma, multiple sclerosis, and tumors.

THE BRAIN AS A METAPHYSICAL TRANSDUCER

And now for one of the most puzzling areas of brain function: If the function of neurons is basically to transmit information, where and how does this information originate?

If we were to use a tiny electrode to apply minute amounts of electricity to various areas of the brain, we could externally activate the neurons in those areas and reproduce a large number of brain functions. We could make a person move an arm; experience pain, pleasure, or fear; hear music; see visions; become angry or anxious; remember a face or experience; have a thought. All of these functions we can obtain by externally stimulating the brain, that is, by having an impulse originate from outside the brain. But how do signals originate from *within* the brain?

Let us explore this phenomenon by looking at a simple situation, such as moving a thumb. The brain contains an area specifically responsible for thumb movement. If we were to electrically stimulate this area, we would bring about movement of the thumb. If a person voluntarily moved the thumb, that area would show increased activity as measured by Position Emission Tomography (*PET*) *scanning*, a technique that measures brain activity. In both situations, the area was stimulated, but what was the source of stimulation in the second case?

Can neurons act not only as transmitters but also as initiators of signals, even if no external physical cause initiated that signal? If a neuron is isolated from all other neurons so that it has no input from other neurons, does it still initiate signals? Certain neurons of the brain do depolarize at a regular rate, but they do so at an automatic, uniform, and predicable rate (i.e., at certain times a second).

The brain contains cells that are the first to fire in response to psychological activity, but the cause-and-effect relationship between psychological and brain activity has never been fully understood. Thinking, a metaphysical activity, has a physical correlate, which is brain activity. But does thinking initiate brain activity, or does brain activity initiate thinking?

In voluntary movement of the thumb, *volition*, a psychological function, was the cause, source, and initiator of brain activity. Volition acted in a similar fashion as the electrode described above. How does volition activate neurons? Volition is not located in the same area of the brain as movement; if a person had a stroke that destroyed the area of the brain responsible for thumb movement, his wanting to move the thumb would not be affected, although he would be unable to perform the movement. In fact, no area in the brain has been correlated with volition, nor are there areas of the brain that have been correlated with any complex emotional activity such as love and hope. There are actually areas of the brain that will become activated if a person *thinks* of moving the thumb, even if he does not carry through with performing the movement, but that still leaves it unclear as to what actually activated that particular area responsible for thinking. It appears that volition, much like electrical stimulation, originates from outside of the brain.

I conceive the brain as a two-way metaphysical transducer, an alchemist transforming metaphysical activities such as thoughts and feelings into electrochemical patterns, and vice versa, converting electrochemical patterns into metaphysical activity. The brain is thus the point of union between the physical and the metaphysical.

Traditional science finds this a very difficult concept. Scientists have concerned themselves with analyzing data that can be measured, and although there are tools to measure electrochemical processes in the brain, there are no tools to measure metaphysical activity. The result of this situation is that the study of the functions of the brain has been delegated to two groups of individuals: those who study physical phenomenon (which includes most neuroscientists) and those who study metaphysical processes, such as philosophers, theologians, psychiatrists, and psychologists. The sad result of this situation is that each group studies its field independent of the other group, leading to further artificial separation between the two.

In the case of brain function, the metaphysical and physical (or electrochemical) activities are not different processes but instead are different expressions of the same thing: human activity. I find it useful to conceptualize this idea as the brain sitting in the middle of two facing mirrors, one reflecting physical and the other metaphysical activity. The brain is the transducer between the two images. Since the images are reflections of each other, a change in one produces an immediate change in the other. But because they reflect each other at all times, it is impossible to detect which image changed first. Utilizing this scheme, there really is no duality between mind and brain; they are different expressions of the same thing.

3 Functional Organization of the Brain

Through our brains, we interact with the external universe. The brain internalizes and processes information about the external world. It also directs our bodies to act in that same world. Both the input and output of the brain are the result of a hierarchical processing of information.

INPUT TO THE BRAIN

Information about the external world is captured in the brain by *receptors*, the doors and windows by which information around us is given access to the brain. Discussed in more detail in the section on perception, receptors are cellular structures that transduce physical information such as light waves, smells, tastes, sounds, and sensory data into electrical impulses, which are then carried by neurons to the brain. Receptors are interesting structures. They take many shapes and forms, but they are highly specialized to transduce only one type (or modality) of information. Thus, receptors for light in the eyes are uniquely shaped and function very differently from those in the ear, which transduce sounds. There are five modalities of information (visual, auditory, gustatory, olfactory, and sensory) and five categories of receptors corresponding to the modalities they capture. By means of receptors, we are able to capture an amazing amount of information about the external world. Although each category of receptor can process only one specific type of information, all receptors, if overstimulated, can transmit the sensation of pain.

The information captured by all receptors, regardless of the modality they capture, is transduced by them into electrochemical impulses that are carried by axons to the brain for proper processing. Information from the body, including the trunk and the extremities, is carried by peripheral nerves to the spinal cord and from there by axons inside the spinal cord. Information from the organs in the head (eyes, ears, tongue, face, etc.) is carried to the brain by cranial nerves, which enter the brainstem, and from there is carried to the brain.

Before reaching the cortex, however, all modalities of information, except for the olfactory, make a stop at the *thalamus*, an egg-shaped structure located below the cortex. The thalamus has an important role in the processing of information. As described in the section on perception, one of the main known functions of the thalamus is to act as a gatekeeper that selects and limits the information that is allowed to reach the cortex. If it was not for the thalamus and associated structures, we would not be able to focus on specific incoming information. The thalamus also allows us to react reflectively to threatening information before the cortex becomes aware of it. Additionally, the thalamus directs the incoming information to the appropriate area in the cortex for it to be processed.

Interestingly, most sensorial information that is carried to the brain is split into two "halves" carried to the opposite side of the brain from its point of origin. For example, touch and temperature sensation from the right side of the body is carried to the left side of the brain. A similar process occurs with vision. If we look straight ahead and divide our field of vision with a vertical line into two equal halves, the left half is carried to the right occipital cortex and vice versa (Figure 3-1). This does not hold as true for other modalities such as smell and taste, which are carried in some degree to both sides of the brain.

From the thalamus, the information is carried on to *primary areas* of the brain. These are certain areas of the brain that are the first to receive the information stemming from the outside world and are thus said to be in direct contact with the external world. As we will learn in the chapter on perception, primary areas are fundamental for the process of perception. Each type or modality of information (i.e., visual, auditory, and other information) is transmitted to and received in separate and specific primary areas of the brain. Thus, there are areas that receive visual, auditory, gustatory, olfactory, and sensory information from the eyes, ears, tongue, nose, and sensory receptors, respectively. Primary areas are *modality specific*, that is, they receive information from only one type of sensory modality. Consequently, damage to these areas results in the loss of the specific sensory modality about which that area receives information. For example, damage to the occipital lobe, where the visual area is located, will result in cortical blindness. Even though in this case there is no abnormality of the eyes, the person is blind because the visual cortex fails to receive information from the eyes.

At some point in this early processing of information by the thalamus and the cortical areas, an interesting process takes place. Information is grouped into what we will call units, with certain boundaries that give the information a specific shape or definition. For example, if we look at a picture on a wall, we are able to discern the limits of the picture, where it starts and ends. If we look straight ahead of us, we see a large variety of objects, each with its own identity. Our brain is able to discern where the

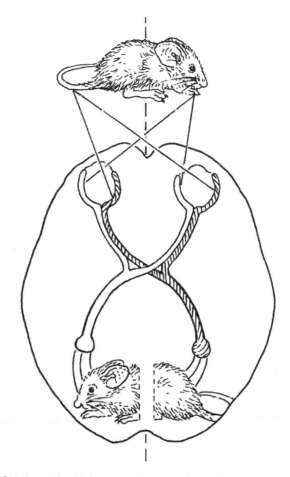

FIGURE 3-1 Splitting of visual information. Objects in the left hemifield are carried to the right occipital cortex and vice versa.

boundaries of each object begin and end, so we can identify each individual object. We are constantly extracting the relevant information from reality, constantly synthesizing, constantly contracting infinity into finitude. If this was not the case, everything we see would be just a blob, devoid of individual components. The same holds true for what we hear. Our brain can group a certain amount of sound waves into a unit that corresponds to one word or one musical piece. The process by which the brain accomplishes this is, to a large degree, unknown.

An important point we ponder in more detail in the section on perception is that the primary cortex is where conscious perception appears to take place. That is to say, that in order for us to *know*, or to be aware, that we are looking at an object, the information regarding that object must travel from the eye and reach the primary cortex.

Primary areas of the brain then send the information to secondary brain areas, which are responsible for grouping information into units and identifying the units' meaning. Secondary areas are still modality specific, responsible for processing information of a single modality. Damage to these areas results in modality-specific deficits. For example, a person may see a lion but be unable to identify it as a lion.

Information from secondary areas of the brain is then transmitted to tertiary areas, which are able to process much more complex information. Tertiary brain areas are able to integrate information stemming from multiple secondary areas and corresponding to different modalities. In the case of an encounter with a lion, the tertiary cortex integrates visual, auditory, and olfactory information pertaining to the lion and comes up with a comprehensive representation (Figure 3-2). Additionally, the tertiary cortex also incorporates information proceeding from what can be called the affective areas of the brain. These areas have a unique role: They impart affective coloring to the bit of information. Every piece of information, everything we come in contact with, everything we perceive in the universe, has two components, a rational constituent and an affective constituent. In short, when we look at an object or hear a word or a song, two kinds of information are imparted by our brain: the physical properties, such as what and where the object or sound is, and the emotional qualities, our feelings about it. Certain areas of the brain are responsible for the emotional component of a bit of information. These areas associate that specific bit of information, such as the "picture" of a lion, with emotional data. Thus, a bit of information once processed by these areas becomes a more complete bit, now also containing emotional data and details. This emotional data stems from past experiences with that bit or similar bits of information. These past experiences do not necessarily result from having encountered that information in the past but could be due to what a person has learned or heard about that information. Some investigators feel that much of the emotional information described here is not learned but is somewhat encoded in our brains; we are afraid of lions even if we have never seen or heard about lions before encountering one.

As we well know, emotion is not just a psychological phenomenon but a psychophysical process. When we see, hear, or experience something that makes us excited, afraid, or happy, our blood pressure and pulse go up and our degree of sweating and gastrointestinal motility increases. The hair in our skin rises; our mouth goes dry. This is all because the areas of the brain involved with emotional coloring are connected to other areas that control our bodily functions.

FIGURE 3-2   Schematic representation of progressive definition of information reaching the brain. As the information is transported to "deeper" areas of the brain, it is given more definition and meaning, as discussed in text.

Although it is highly likely that one's entire body and brain participate in the emotional experience, there are areas of the brain that appear to have an important role in both the subjective feeling and objective expression of emotion. These areas include, but are not limited to, the paralimbic and limbic areas and the hypothalamus.

The *limbic system* is composed of a number of interconnected structures that are involved in learning, memory, and emotion. Within the limbic system is a particular series of interconnected structures that constitute the Papez circuit, named after the American neurologist James Papez. This "circuit" comprises areas of the brain, including the cingulate cortex, the hippocampus, the hypothalamus, and the anterior nuclei of the thalamus. Many scientists believe that intercommunication between structures of this circuit plays a fundamental role in the emotional experience, although others have questioned this concept.

Other areas of the brain appear to have a particular role in the link between the mental and visceral expression of emotion. Among these areas are the insula and the hypothalamus. It is thought that other cortical areas of the brain send impulses to these areas, resulting in the visceral components of emotion. In experimental situations using animals and humans, electrical stimulation by means of an electrode applied to these areas resulted in changes in blood pressure, gastrointestinal motility, sweating, and even cardiac arrest. This explains why some individuals exposed to a strong emotional experience can experience death from cardiac arrest. It also explains why patients suffering from seizures involving these areas of the brain frequently complain of visceral manifestations during the seizure, since a seizure is, in fact, excessive electrical activity. More on these areas is discussed in the chapter on the autonomic nervous system.

THE FINAL CORTICAL REPRESENTATION

After processing information received by receptors, nerves, the thalamus, the cortex, and other areas of the brain, the cortical representation of an object we have encountered in the universe is thus complete. The cortical representation is not a mirror image of the object, such as that which would be captured by a camera. The physical reality pertaining to an object in the universe is transduced by the brain into an electrochemical force that contains much more than details about its physical characteristics. It also contains an affective component, which is unique to each person's history.

There is yet another fundamental difference between a mirror's and our brain's reflection of outside reality. The mirror's reflection lasts only for the time that the object is in front of it. The object makes no changes in the structure of the mirror; the mirror does not remember or keep a record of the images it reflects. The brain does. As discussed in sections on learning, memory, and brain plasticity, the brain is structurally changed by its interaction with the outside world. Whatever we come in contact with in the outside universe has the potential to permanently change us.

OUTPUT OF THE BRAIN: HUMAN MOVEMENT

The output of the brain to the external world is manifested in terms of movement. The elementary process by which we act upon the universe occurs through our ability to move. Our thoughts can change the world, but if we are unable to convey our thoughts to others by means of spoken or written words or by any other modality that involves movement, we will become prisoners within ourselves and be unable to act upon the universe outside of ourselves. The movement of one's mouth and tongue, an extremely complex and exact form of movement, forms the words that convey a message. The complex movement of one's hands and fingers allows one to write or draw. The movement within an organism, even the movement of internal organs or that of molecules across cellular membranes, is the indicator of life. When movement stops, so does life.

The coordination and initiation of movement by all of our voluntary muscles stem from the brain. Movement is also organized in the brain in a hierarchical fashion, much as is input into the brain. Primary motor areas are responsible for moving individual muscles, or more often, small groups of muscles. If we were to electrically stimulate those areas, we could bring about movement of small areas such as a finger or a hand. These primary areas of the brain receive their stimulation from secondary motor areas, which are responsible for more complex movements, such as walking or playing an instrument. These more complex movements are a result of a number of muscle groups working in exact coordination. These secondary motor areas send impulses to multiple primary areas, which results in movement of multiple muscle groups or areas. Yet other areas are responsible for very complex movements, such as coordinating the hands or the mouth for production of verbal or written language. These areas are called *tertiary areas* because they in turn control both secondary and primary motor areas.

The control of bodily movement by the brain is organized in a hierarchical fashion. At the top of this hierarchy are groups of neurons that are responsible for planning movement. These neurons send orders to other neurons in the hierarchy until the order is received by neurons in the primary motor cortex, which are responsible for the movement of the individual muscles. Consider the analogy of a giant ship that is propelled by thousands of rowers. At one end of the ship is the admiral, at the other end the individual rowers. The admiral decides that he wants the ship to reach point A. Utilizing feedback data from the weather and water conditions, he devises a plan as to how to get to point A and gives the order to his lieutenant, who works out some of the details of the journey. The lieutenant gives orders to the petty officers, who are each responsible for a group of rowers.

Some important points in this analogy pertain to the brain and movement. First, the actual movement is performed by the oars, which are moved by the rowers. Neither the admiral nor the lieutenants or petty officers have oars, and thus they do not row. The rowers only follow orders imparted by officers above them and know little about the admiral's plan.

Their orders come from those immediately above them, such as the petty officers, and not from the admiral himself, who is concerned about the big picture of the journey and not about its details. If some of the rowers become unable to row because of death or sickness, the boat could, depending on the number of remaining rowers, continue moving, although in an impaired fashion.

At the other end of the chain of command, the admiral is responsible for planning the journey but does not concern himself with the details. His contact is with the officers below him, to whom he imparts his orders. As the orders descend in the hierarchy of command, further details are worked out, such as which section of rowers should row at each time to maintain the desired direction. If the admiral dies or gets sick and it becomes unable to impart orders, the ship would not move, since only he knows the direction of where to go. The same pertains to his officers. Depending on their position in the hierarchy, their deaths could impair or stop the movement of the ship. The rowers could still row, but the lack of coordination and orders from those above them would make their rowing useless.

Applying this analogy to the brain, the rowers are neurons within the primary motor cortex. These neurons are responsible for the movement of individual muscles. The admiral represents the higher association motor cortex. Within these two groups of neurons are other groups that in an hierarchical fashion plan and coordinate the movement to be performed and send orders down the line of hierachical command until they reach the rowers. In our ship example, the admiral and other officers have little if any contact with the lower officers and the rowers. Likewise, the higher association motor cortex has few connections with the primary cortex.

An important concept to grasp is that at all levels of this naval hierarchy, feedback is utilized to modify the particular functions performed at each section. The admiral, the officers below him, and even the rowers utilize information they obtain about weather conditions, position of the ship, and so on to modify their actions. Similarly, all levels of the cortical hierarchy responsible for movement utilize information stemming from sensory organs to constantly modify their actions. The thalamus has an important role in this process by transmitting information from the sensory areas of the brain to the pertinent motor areas, thus allowing for constant feedback so motor areas can adjust their functions appropriately.

The naval analogy is also useful to explain how damage to the brain at different levels affects function. As stated, death of the admiral would severely impair movement of the ship. Those below him, such as the rowers, are still able to perform their functions but only in an uncoordinated fashion. Similarly, in the brain, damage to higher association motor areas, such as that responsible for language output, makes speaking impossible, even though the individual neurons of the primary cortex responsible for movement of the mouth and tongue are intact. On the other extreme of the hierarchy, the death of rowers would affect the movement of the ship, depending on how many rowers are affected and where in the ship they are located. The death of a small number of rowers located in a key area for movement of the ship could have serious consequences. Likewise, damage to primary areas of the brain impairs function to the degree of the number of neurons damaged and their location. If damage occurs to areas of the brain affecting some areas responsible for movement of the tongue and mouth while leaving others intact, a person may still be able to speak.

Within this hierarchy of the brain system responsible for movements are certain groups of neurons with particular functions. The cerebellum has an important role in the maintenance of equilibrium and balance and coordination of movements, including gait. As with all other functions of the brain, smooth movements result from the harmonious balance of two opposing and complementary forces—in the case of movement, the balance between the contraction of agonist and antagonist muscles. For example, if while I am sitting down I move my wrist from my knee to my face, some muscles (the agonist muscles) are moving my wrist in the direction of the face and other muscles, (the antagonistic muscles) are opposing those muscles so that movement is not overly rapid or brusque. The cerebellum has an important role in the balance between the two groups. Thus, damage to the cerebellum results in ataxia, the loss of smoothness in muscle movement. Gait is also frequently affected by cerebellum damage.

The basal ganglia also have an important role in the initiation and other poorly understood components of movement. Their importance can be appreciated by the severe abnormalities in movement exhibited by patients suffering from basal ganglia disorders.

In conclusion, the ability of the brain to perceive and to act upon the world results from harmonious actions of a number of its areas.

4 Brain Plasticity, Intelligence, and Learning

BRAIN PLASTICITY

As I was returning corrected examinations to medical students a few weeks ago, I remarked that the answers given to the questions on the exam showed evidence that plastic changes had taken place in the students' brains. One particularly outspoken disciple stood up and remarked that it was beneath a professor of my stature to insult students by claiming that their brains were made of plastic and that their poor performances on the exam were most likely a reflection of my second-rate didactic techniques. I answered that in fact all the students' performances on the exam had been excellent and my comments were meant to indicate that the material had been well learned. Without the least degree of hesitation, the same student remarked that he had been only joking and that the excellent scores obtained by students were a reflection of my excellent pedagogical methodology.

One of the most exciting discoveries in neurosciences in recent years is in the area of *brain plasticity*, a term coined to designate the enormous malleability of the brain. In fact, we now know that the brain is far from being the static structure it was felt to be a few decades back. Instead, the brain is an ever-changing system, constantly modifying its physical and functional architecture in response to its interaction with the universe that surrounds it and in response to changes that take place within itself.

A number of important points can be made about our current state of knowledge of brain plasticity. First, brain plasticity does not consist of a single type of morphological change but in fact encompasses many different processes that take place throughout the lifetime of an individual and involves participation by virtually all of the cellular constituents of the brain, including neurons, glia, vascular, and other types of cells. Brain plasticity involves morphologic changes within individual cells and in the connections between cells, so that there is both an *intracellular* as well as an *intercellular* component. Because, as we have discussed in prior sections, the brain is a system composed by billions of cells that are connected and in constant interaction with each other, it seems readily evident that changes to any of its cellular components will result in a change in the system as a whole. However, at any one moment in time and depending on a number of factors, plastic changes may predominate in certain areas of the brain over other areas.

Second, brain plasticity has a clear age-dependent determinant. This determinant includes both the degree and the type of structural and functional changes that take place in the brain. Specific types of plasticity predominate during certain periods of an individual's lifetime and either do not take place or are less prominent at other times. Therefore, "time windows" exist for certain types of plasticity, which means that if they do not take place in an individual during a precise period of time, they may not take place at all. For example, *pruning*, a form of plasticity discussed in more detail in subsequent sections, occurs mainly during childhood and not at other times. This type of plasticity may account for functions such as language development.

Third, other inter-individual differences, apart from age, determine the degree and type of plastic changes an individual experiences. Gender, for example, seems to play an important role.

Last, the changes in brain morphology and function encompassed by the term brain plasticity occur within two different arenas: in the context of normal brain development and as an adaptive mechanism to maximize functional abilities (or to make maximal use of the remaining intact brain) in the presence of brain injury. There are many commonalties in the types of change that occur in both situations, but there are also many differences, not the least of which is the initiator and purpose for those changes. In the case of normal brain development, plastic changes constitute the underlying physiological correlate for such functions as learning, memory, language development, development of motor and non-motor skills, and virtually any change in or addition to the functional abilities for which the brain is responsible. Thus, in the course of learning how to play the piano, the brain cells responsible for moving the fingers will change as the person learns. An increase in the complexity of cells responsible for moving the fingers as well as in the connections within cells constitute, at least in part, the underlying neuronal representation for learning how to play the piano.

Plasticity and Brain Repair

In the course of brain repair, plastic changes are geared toward maximizing function in spite of the damaged brain. An example of brain plasticity initiated by injury is the following: When the area in the brain responsible for moving the right limb in a rat is damaged, brain cells surrounding the injured area will undergo a change in their function and morphology that will allow them to take on the functions of the damaged cells. The effectiveness of these plastic changes depends on a number of factors, such as the animal's age.

Although this phenomenon is not as well studied in man, rapidly emerging scientific data indicates that similar (although less effective) changes occur in human brains following injury. Following injury to a particular area of the human brain, it appears that other areas will change their characteristics to take on the functions of the damaged area. This form of brain plasticity is much more effective at an early age. Infants who suffer damage to the brain area responsible for language, for example, maintain the capacity to develop language, but they do so by utilizing areas other than the damaged brain areas. Gender also has an important role in brain plasticity. Thus, in the case of brain damage to areas of the brain responsible for language, girls are able to retain the capacity to develop other areas of the brain for language until a later age than do boys.

The search for potential strategies to augment brain plasticity initiated by injury promises to yield important therapeutic tools to be used in the remediation of brain injury. More on these issues is discussed in subsequent sections.

Plasticity and Brain Development

Plastic changes that occur accompanying normal brain development have received a great deal of scientific interest in recent decades. The notion that the physical characteristics of the brain constantly change throughout an individual's lifetime is not an entirely new concept, but what was not well understood until recently are the factors that initiate those changes and the type and degree of modifications that take place. Even more, only recently have studies shown the immense importance of an individual's interaction with the environment in determining the characteristics of brain plasticity.

This is not to say that interplay with the environment is the sole determinant for changes that occur in the morphology of the brain throughout an individual's lifetime. To be sure, a multiplicity of other factors, such as genetic and programmed changes, occur with aging. Additionally, genetic and programmed factors themselves probably play a significant role in determining the degree of brain plasticity that occurs secondary to environmental interaction.

To better understand the role of the environment in determining brain plasticity, let's examine the following point: Interaction with the environment implies two processes. The first is the exposure to and receipt of information *from* the environment, and the second is *acting upon* that same environment. It appears that each of these processes initiates a specific type of plastic change that takes place in the brain. From recent discoveries in brain plasticity, we are now able to make the following somewhat daring affirmation: In addition to a multitude of other factors such as genetic influences, the brain is shaped both by the characteristics of the environment to which an individual is exposed and by the characteristics of the actions committed by that same individual.

How does the receipt of information from the environment influence brain plasticity? Let us explore this question further.

A fascinating feature of neurons is that they need a purpose to survive; without a purpose, neurons will literally commit suicide through a process called *apoptosis*, which is sort of the neuronal equivalent to ritual *hara-kiri*. Apoptosis, or self-induced death of neurons, occurs in a number of other situations, including infections, aging, brain tumors, and a variety of disorders that cause a disruption in the normal function of the neuron. Rather than surrender itself to function in an abnormal fashion, the neuron virtually kills itself, using its own genetic material to self-destruct when it recognizes an abnormality. A similar situation occurs with loss of purpose. We have discussed that the main purpose of neurons is to communicate with other neurons; that is to say, to receive signals from certain neurons and send a signal to other neurons down the line. Neurons deprived of the ability to either receive or transmit information to other neurons will become damaged or die (Figure 4-1).

A well-studied case of neuronal death secondary to absence of input is that which occurs when newborn kittens are placed in a dark room or have their eyelids sewn shut, so that they are prevented from receiving light input. Within a few weeks, the occipital cortex of those cats will degenerate in an irreversible fashion. Even if re-exposed to light at a later time, the animals will remain cortically blind, which means that even though visual information reaches the brain because of intact eyes and visual pathways, the neurons in the brain responsible for processing visual information have undergone degeneration and are unable to do so.

Loss of purpose does not refer only to the neuron as a whole; it can also include connections with other neurons. That is to say, when specific connections between neurons are not utilized, those connections, rather than the entire neuron, will degenerate. Recent research has demonstrated that the brain creates an excess of connections in the context of normal development. Thus, the brain of a four to eight-year-old child contains a very large number of connections, many more so than the brain of an older child. It seems that in the process of normal growth, some of those connections are "pruned," much as a gardener prunes a bush to give it the desired

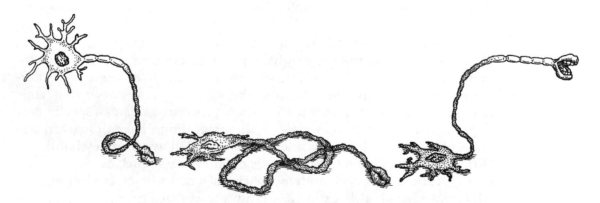

FIGURE 4-1   Death of a neuron results in death of both the neuron from which it receives information and the neuron to which it sends information.

shape. What determines the shape of the neuronal bush? Data that is rapidly accumulating suggests that those connections utilized by means of experience or exposure will survive, while those not utilized will die. This overproduction and subsequent selection of synapses occurring secondary to environmental exposure appears to be one of the most important mechanisms of brain plasticity, allowing for "custom building" of the brain. This does not mean that two children exposed to exactly the same environment will develop the same pattern of brain development, since as we stated before, a multitude of other factors can determine the type and degree of plastic changes that will occur secondary to environmental exposure.

Additional support for this theory stems from a recent study that utilized a technique called PET scanning to quantify brain activity in children at different ages. This study showed that the brain consumes the most energy and therefore is most active from ages four to eight years, which corresponds to the age groups in which there are the greatest numbers of synapses or connections between neurons. Both energy consumption and number of synapses decrease after that age. Neuroscientists have suggested that the reason for this increased energy consumption is that from ages four to eight, the brain is most receptive to stimulation from the external world. Those areas of the brain that are stimulated during that time will remain as they are or develop further, and those areas not stimulated will decrease the number of synapses, and therefore decrease energy consumption. It's the old "what you don't use, you lose" situation. Proponents of this theory point out that people with certain skills, such as musicians or artists, have gotten prominent stimulation in those topics during those ages. Similarly, children who learn a language during those ages and later forget or fail to use it have a much better ability to relearn that language later. This phenomenon is theoretically due to the fact that the area of the brain responsible for that language becomes more developed when the child learns the language and remains developed during the individual's lifetime, even if that language is not used after it is learned.

The role of the environment in determining the morphology of the brain was recently demonstrated by a scientific experiment that compared the brains of a group of rats reared in a complex (highly colorful and stimulating) environment with the brains of another group of rats reared in a "dull" environment. The occipital cortex of the rats in the first group showed increased synaptic size as well as greater number of synapses per neuron and number of astrocytes per neuron.

Another type of plasticity is the creation of new connections secondary to need. For example, "forced" motor activity has a prominent role in brain plasticity. An animal that is forced to overuse one particular limb because the limb in the opposite side is tied down will develop new connections in the area of the brain that is responsible for moving the free limb. We presume that a similar process takes place with the use of other brain functions (Figures 4-2 and 4-3). The greater use of a particular brain function results in a greater degree of complexity (including a greater number of connections) in the area of the brain responsible for that particular function.

Evidence for brain plasticity secondary to motor activity in humans is beginning to rapidly accumulate. For example, scientists discovered that

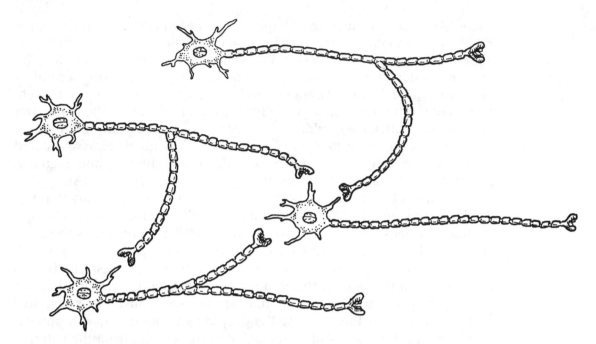

FIGURES 4-2 AND 4-3   The process of "sprouting." New connections between neurons are built (or "sprouted") according to need. Figure 4-2 indicates the baseline; Figure 4-3 represents the same number of neurons but with extra connections between them.

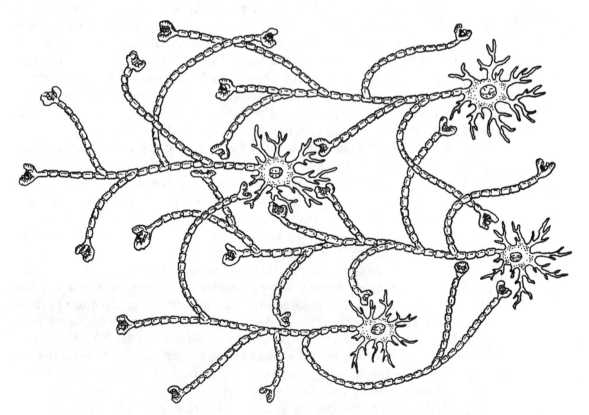

FIGURE 4-3

the area of the brain responsible for moving the fingers of the left hand in six accomplished violin players was larger than the area responsible for the fingers of the right hand, which are used less in playing the violin. The difference in size of that area of the brain was greater in the violinists who had begun playing at an early age. Additionally, violinists had larger brain areas dedicated to moving the fingers of either hand than did people who could not play the violin. A conclusion from this finding is that greater use of the left than the right fingers in violin players led to higher development of the brain areas responsible for moving the left fingers. Greater use of all fingers in violinists as opposed to non-violinists led to greater development of brain areas responsible for finger movement in the former group.

Changes in brain morphology brought on by certain behaviors possibly applies to more than just motor functions and includes more complex behavior patterns. A simple example of this phenomenon was demonstrated in an experiment performed in lobsters, where infant individuals were placed in one of two aquariums; in one, there were peaceful lobsters, and in the other, aggressive and larger animals (yes, lobsters do have personalities). Lobster infants placed with aggressive peers tended to develop a greater of the amygdala (which is the area of the brain believed to play a prominent role in aggression) than the group placed with more placid brothers. Although it is dangerous to extrapolate to humans the results of experiments performed in animals, some investigators have suggested that the same phenomenon could hold true for intellectual and even behavioral development in children; stimulation at an early age could bring about plastic changes in the brain, manifested by increased development of areas responsible for intellectual or certain behavioral functions. Thus, the performance of certain behavioral patterns may result in the establishment of neuronal patterns that will further engrain that same behavior. This brings us to one of the most remarkable points about brain plasticity and brain function. The brain is both the source and the effect of human activity. In the case of the violin players, the brain initiates (is the source of) the movement of the fingers, but with time, the increased use of those fingers will act on the brain itself to cause greater development of those same cells that are responsible for the movement.

The concept of brain plasticity has enormous implications. Changes in the architecture of the brain secondary to stimulation and demands from the external environment represent an anatomical substrate for behavior. "One becomes as one does," states the Talmud. The wisdom contained in this 1,500-year-old statement is dazzling. Behavior is not isolated; it cannot be separated from a person's internal structure. If one "does," or behaves, a certain way, a person's internal structure will be in accordance with their behavior. Since behavior is localized in the nervous system, this concept can be applied to the brain. This is the essence of the concept of brain plasticity. Behavior reflects structure, and structure reflects behavior—mirror images of each other.

Through this process of pruning of unused connections, and creation of required new connections, the brain is, at least in part, custom shaped to our needs.

INTELLIGENCE

How intelligent are you? Let us attempt to answer this question by giving you a seemingly simple test. Define the word *intelligence*. If you are gasping for an answer, hold on tight to your overalls and do not despair. You are not alone. Most people, including neuroscientists, have a great deal of difficulty in defining this word. Intelligence is a little like dreams and UFOs—everybody knows about them, but nobody knows exactly what they are.

Perhaps the most accepted definition of intelligence is "the ability to deal adaptively with a changing environment, to benefit from past experience, to proceed in goal-directed fashion, to pursue productive avenues of problem solving and to exclude dead ends, and most important, to perceive common properties in otherwise separate domains of experience." As with other unclear concepts about any field, long definitions usually indicate a lack of clear understanding about the concept. A shorter, more workable definition of intelligence could be "our ability to utilize what we know, perceive, and foresee to find adequate solutions to problems." Intelligence is not a single brain function, but in fact, it is made up of a series of other activities such as learning, memory, and an extremely sophisticated indexing and retrieval system that can link significant events from past experience and apply them to the solution of a current problem.

Far from being a straightforward notion, intelligence is a vague and elusive concept, especially if one tries to quantify and measure it. For example, problem-solving ability is the primordial component of intelligence, but in many instances there is clearly more than one way of reaching a solution and more than one solution to a problem. Cultural, socioeconomic, and individual influences could certainly have an impact on an individual's particular manner of arriving at a solution. For a person making up a test that measures problem-solving ability, determining the most adequate answer to a problem often becomes a subjective decision. This has led to much controversy in the definition and, most important, the measurement of intelligence. In fact, most tests of intelligence compare a person's performance to that of a reference group, which in the United States consists of white, middle-class individuals. Many critics of these tests allude to social, cultural, and economic biases built into them.

Intelligence is not localized to any one area of the brain; in fact, its components are distributed through multiple zones. All organisms have some form of intelligence, but there is a significant difference in the degree of intelligence among species. To expand on this topic, let me relate a true story. During a recent verbal altercation I had with an unknown motorist, he proceeded to call me a squid brain. After giving the matter some thought, I politely asked my aggressor to expand on the meaning of his comment. Although somewhat taken aback by my question, he answered that it appeared to him that my dumb behavior could only result from me having a brain the size and shape of a squid brain. I had to humbly bow my head in respect for this fellow's profound knowledge of neurophysiology and neurophylegeny (the evolution of the nervous system). He was correct in his assertion that among species there is a clear difference in the size and, most important, the structure of the brain and that this difference highly correlates with what we perceive as the intelligence of the species. Thus, utilizing our criteria and measure of intelligence, most squids tend to be less intelligent than most humans, and a large proportion of humans (excepting politicians and certain attorneys of my acquaintance) have more developed brains than the majority of squids.

What differentiates the brains of species with higher and lower intelligence is not the absolute weight of the brain but the size of the brain in relation to the size of the body and, most important, the complexity of the structure of the brain. We believe that species with a higher brain/body ratio are more intelligent.

Complexity in the structure of the brain, including the type and number of neurons and number of synapses, also highly correlates with intelligence of a species. As a rule, areas of the brain that are responsible for elaborate behaviors and functions are more complex and developed in species that we perceive as "smarter." For example, species that we believe to be more intelligent have a higher development of the frontal lobes, an area responsible for complex psychological characteristics and activities, including personality, drive, and problem-solving capabilities. Similar differences can be seen in size and structure of areas involving language, memory and learning. These differences in size and weight can be accounted for by the number, type, and size of neurons and glial cells, and, perhaps more crucial, by the difference in the number of synapses.

It is interesting to note that certain cetaceans, in particular dolphins, have a brain size and body/brain ratio nearly the same as humans and in fact exceed humans in the complexity of brain structure. The significance of this finding in respect to the intelligence of dolphins is unclear.

For many years scientists have attempted to elucidate whether there is any difference between the brains of smart and not-so-smart individuals within the same species. Thus, much energy has been devoted to examining the brains of people such as Einstein, and indeed there are some vague and questionable reports of a higher number of glial cells but not of neurons in a certain area of his brain. Overall, however, the search has been disappointing, and no conclusive difference between an intelligent and a less clever squid or human, or between politicians and other individuals, has been found. This, however, probably is due to our lack of knowledge about the type of differences we should look for, rather than from the absence of such differences.

What Determines Our Intelligence?

The definitive answer to this question is unknown, but it probably involves a combination of genetic factors (how much intelligence is encoded in our genes) and environmental factors (what our brain is subjected to while in our mother's womb and after birth). Clearly, we can do little about genetic factors but much about environmental elements.

In regard to genetic factors, it appears that intelligence is, to a degree, inherited, but how much so is not well understood. Although a number of scientific studies have examined this matter, many of them are controversial and their results difficult to interpret.

Environmental factors that have an impact on an individual's intelligence can be divided into pre- and postbirth. The brain begins to form shortly after conception and continues to develop during most of gestation, or pregnancy. During that period of time, the developing brain has certain requirements, such as proper nutrition, which must be met for satisfactory development. Also during those months, the brain is highly vulnerable to noxious influences, and excessive exposure by the mother to such elements as alcohol, certain prescription and recreational drugs, tobacco, and toxin will affect brain development and have a prominent impact on the child's intelligence. Certain conditions in the pregnant mother, including infections and chronic disease, can also affect a child's mental capacity. Decreased oxygenation of the brain due to a difficult birth process has also been frequently associated with subsequent intellectual deficits in the child.

What is the influence of the postbirth environment on the development of a person's intelligence? Although much of the vast amount of scientific data on this subject is controversial and difficult to interpret, there is clear evidence that behavioral stimulation, social situation, motivational factors, emotional stability, presence of adequate role models, degree of opportunity, and other poorly classified factors have very important roles in the development of intelligence. Additionally, as we have discussed, research in recent years has demonstrated that there is a certain "time window," or period of time during which the brain is very "plastic." This means that during that period the brain is malleable and, if properly stimulated by means of incoming information, will increase its structural complexity, resulting in intellectual growth. This increased plasticity is present during a limited amount of time. Failure to take advantage of it by stimulating the brain during that period could conceivably have a permanent deleterious effect on an individual's subsequent degree of intelligence.

An excellent example of the role of the environment on intelligence was provided by an experiment performed in the 1960s, in which a number of orphans diagnosed with mental retardation were placed in a state institution at a very early age. Most of these children profited so much from the extra play and care they received that they reportedly became "normally intelligent," were put up for adoption, and grew up to become self-supporting, middle-class adults. This group of children was compared to another group of the same age who were initially of normal intelligence and who had been left in an orphanage where the infants received little individual attention. After a number of years, intelligence testing revealed a gain in IQ points in the children placed in the state institution and a significant drop in the IQ points of the children who remained in the orphanage. In fact, one of the children who remained in the orphanage and who initially was of normal intelligence became severely retarded by age 19. Although this is an extreme case, numerous studies have reported that stimulation at an early age has a prominent impact on the subsequent development of intelligence.

The examples of brain plasticity we have examined refer to very specific areas of the brain, including those that control aggression, music, and language. We have already mentioned, however, that intelligence does not have a single localization and is widespread throughout many areas of the brain. Brain plasticity, or changes in the brain that lead to greater intelligence, would, therefore, theoretically need to take place in multiple brain areas and would be more difficult to document in research studies.

LEARNING AND MEMORY

We have seen that there is a prominent temporal determinant to certain types of brain plasticity and that the brain appears to be more plastic during certain ages. A large proportion of the readers of this book will be somewhat past this window of opportunity and will wonder what's left for them. Our earlier statements in no way mean that we cannot improve our intelligence after childhood. Brain plasticity continues throughout the lifetime of an individual, although the type and degree of plasticity change over time. Learning, and thus increasing our knowledge base, also continues during much of an individual's lifetime, and since intelligence is highly dependent on our ability to retrieve learned information and apply it to the solution of a particular problem, increasing our knowledge in part increases our intelligence. Problem-solving techniques, another component of intelligence, can also be learned throughout one's lifetime.

But how is it that we learn? How does the brain code, store, and retrieve information? What changes are brought about in the brain when we learn new material? If I learn a set of 10 numbers, how is my brain different from a few minutes ago, prior to learning them? When I master a foreign language or a musical instrument or even a new profession, how is my brain modified? These are some of the most baffling questions plaguing neuroscientists, and although the answers are far from clear, some headway into these queries has been made in recent years.

For many years it was felt that neurons would "write down," or encode, learned information to be remembered by creating new molecules, very much as a person would use a special code to inscribe data in a computer to be recalled later. According to this theory, neurons would decode, or "read," these molecules containing our memories when we needed to recall information. Scientists also theorized that the molecular codes corresponding to specific learned information could be extracted from one individual and transferred to the brain of another individual. To prove this point, scientists in the 1960s performed an interesting and surprising experiment. A group of rats was taught to perform certain tasks. Afterward the animals were sacrificed, and areas of their brains were blended and injected into rats that did not know how to perform the tasks. Rats that received this brain extract reportedly learned to perform the tasks much faster than rats that did not receive it. These experiments led to much excitement within the scientific and nonscientific community. Many thought that the day would come when knowledge would be packaged into capsules or injections containing the molecular codes for all types of information. For example, following this theory, you could have received this manual in a convenient capsule form that if swallowed, would free you from needing to read its hundreds of pages to learn its contents. But like many findings in science that promise to revolutionize a field, multiple similar experiments in animals performed by other investigators failed to reproduce the same results, and the molecular theory of memory was abandoned in the 1970s. It is now felt that memory is not stored in molecules but instead in circuits within the brain.

There appear to be at least two types of modifications that occur in the brain with learning and memory. The first involves changes in the internal structure of neurons, most notably in the area of the synapses. The second consists of an increase in the *number* of synapses, or connections between neurons. These two types of changes are not independent of each other but are most likely interrelated. Modifications in the internal structure of neurons possibly leads to an increase in the number of synapses, and vice versa. It would seem, however, that change in the number of synapses is not a rapid occurrence and probably takes days or weeks to occur. Thus, it could not possibly account for such situations as recalling a telephone number two hours after it's memorized. Cellular changes, on the other hand, can occur much faster and probably account for rapid learning. A continuum between both types of modifications, where cellular changes initially occur and are later followed by an increase in the number of synapses, leading to solidification of learning, is also possible and likely.

The result of these two types of modifications that occur in the brain in response to learning is an improvement in the connectivity between neurons. There is both an enhancement in the efficiency of communication, that is, in the ease by which cells communicate with each other, and an increase in the number of interconnected cells. Thus the brain, the alchemist, is able to change or encode all of our memories into neuronal circuits and to retrieve memories from those circuits when needed.

How long does it take for these cellular changes to take place in response to learning? In certain types of learning, not very long at all. To illustrate this point, let me relate a true story. A few years ago I returned from a trip to Paris carrying on the plane a pair of incredibly smelly goat cheeses that had been given to me by a well-intentioned colleague. After placing the cheeses in the overhead compartment, I noticed that my fellow passengers were tactfully sniffing, staring suspiciously and accusingly at the other passengers around their seats. To conceal my guilt, I did exactly the same thing. Out of politeness and perhaps embarrassment, nobody made any comments. Half an hour later, I asked the person sitting next to me whether she smelled anything unusual, but she looked at me in a strange and condescending (but almost compassionate) manner, as if to say, "You must be really in bad shape if you need to resort to such a bizarre pickup line. What smell are you talking about?" In fact, I noticed that all of my neighbors were either reading or sleeping, and nobody seemed to be concerned by the smell any longer. Only when people walking on the aisle en route to the bathroom approached our location would they begin the looking-around-and-sniffing routine.

This curious situation is a perfect example of a phenomenon called *habituation*, which is one of the simplest and fastest forms of learning. The smell continued to be present in its full intensity throughout the length of the flight, but brain cells quickly learned to identify it as a nonthreatening stimulus and stopped responding to it, so that the conscious brain eventually lost interest in it. This contrasts with *sensitization*, another simple form of learning, in which the brain quickly learns to identify a stimulus as threatening and learns to respond appropriately. For example, if I get pinched in the arm in such an intensity that it produces pain, a second pinch of the same intensity would result in a greater response than the first reaction. My brain cells will learn almost immediately to respond appropriately to a pinch. Both habituation and sensitization are a result of changes in the internal structure of neurons, most likely at the level of the synapse, which occur within seconds or minutes from the time information is presented to the brain cells.

Most learning, however, is much more complex and involves a number of mechanisms for storing and retrieving information. Learned information is initially kept in a short-term memory storage place; after a certain period of time, usually of a few minutes, it gets stored in a longer-term, more permanent memory storage site. How this transition from short- to long-term memory occurs is not well known, but we do know that long-term storage represents a more permanent physical change in neurons, as we discussed in terms of brain modifications. The analogy can be made to what occurs when we enter information in a computer equipped with an AutoSave function. Only after information is saved by storing it on the hard disk, which represents a physical encoding on the hard drive, does the information become permanent. Turning off the computer prior to saving the information will result in lost data. Similarly, a person who loses consciousness will not remember any events that took place for the five minutes prior to blacking out, since that information did not get coded in the long-term memory stores. This explains why an individual involved in a situation such as a car accident, in which he or she loses consciousness, does not remember what took place for a few minutes prior to the accident, as well as fails to recall details about the accident itself.

Declarative and Nondeclarative Learning

There are two types of learning and memory: declarative and nondeclarative. *Declarative memory* refers to the conscious recall of information or events to which we have been exposed in the past. To recall such information, we need to declare, or narrate, that memory verbally or through other means, such as visualizing or thinking about it. In contrast, *nondeclarative memory* refers to the recall of how to perform a procedure, such as riding a bicycle, or the performance of any other skill. On performance of that activity, we do not need to consciously think about how to do it. The expression of nondeclarative learning is through performing something rather than recalling of an event.

There are a number of differences between these two types of memory. First, information storage in each type takes place in different areas of the brain; declarative memories are stored mainly in and around the temporal lobes, while nondeclarative memories are stored in multiple areas of the brain. That is why, when patients lose declarative memory from an event such as a head injury, they usually retain the capacity to perform activities and learn new skills.

But perhaps the greatest difference between both types of memory is the following: Both declarative and nondeclarative memories are encoded through the process of brain plasticity, which results in the brain modifications we discussed. However, brain plasticity for declarative memories remains relatively constant throughout a person's life (except for the elderly), but plasticity for acquisition of nondeclarative memories is most operative during early childhood, as discussed in the section on intelligence. That means that the maximum capacity for acquisition of skills such as playing a musical instrument, speaking a foreign language, and solving problems is during early childhood. As explained, this heightened state of plasticity lasts for only a few years, providing a heightened window of opportunity.

Is there a limit to the amount of information that can be learned? Is the brain similar to a hard disk in a computer that is able to maintain only a certain, limited amount of information? It does not appear to be so.

The brain is clearly a dynamic organ. We are constantly learning new information that gets coded into structural changes in the brain, so the architecture of the brain is being modified at all times. Our ability to learn information and, therefore, for that modification to take place appears to be limitless, although many factors, such as age, limit the speed and degree of learning, as we discuss in subsequent chapters on the brain and aging. Indeed, brain plasticity, the ability of the brain to change its structure and function, decreases with age. This holds true for learning as well as for brain repair after injury. However, under normal circumstances, excluding certain disease states such as dementia, the ability to learn never stops altogether throughout an individual's lifetime.

How much information can a single or a specified number of neurons and neuronal connections hold? If I remember a recent trip to Italy, the plane ride, the cities and sights, the food I ate, the smells of the marketplace, the feelings of excitement and wonder that I experienced, the conversations I had with people I met, how many cells or how many connections between cells does it take to hold the memories of that trip? Is it one, or thousands, or millions? Are the memories of the sights, the smells, the tastes, and the emotions stored in different cells, or all in the same cell under the category "trip to Italy"? And if each cell is able to hold a portion of the memories, how does each cell "release" its memories in perfect sequence so that it all comes together when I recall the trip? These are questions to which we have no clear answers, although we can make some assertions.

First, there appears to be a temporal compartmentalization to storage of memory. In other words, all memories corresponding to events that took place during certain time frames are stored together. Therefore, when patients suffer discrete damage to certain areas of the brain that are involved in memory storage, they frequently lose memory for a certain time frame. For example, patients who suffer head injuries can lose all memories for the prior year but are able to remember events that took place before that time. Interestingly, the older memories are the ones that are stored more "firmly" and thus are more likely to be remembered. This explains why many older patients are able to remember events that took place during their childhoods, but they cannot remember things that took place during recent years or even yesterday.

Second, there appears to be certain categorization to memory storage. This means that information is stored under categories. For example, certain lesions in the brain can result in a patient being unable to recall certain categories of objects such as the names of fruits or tools or even animals. Some patients can lose the ability to remember familiar faces. A patient I mentioned in another section of this book could not remember or identify the faces of family members but could recognize their voices.

Why are some individuals able to remember and learn more and faster than others? Are their neurons more efficient in coding and retrieving information? Or is it that everybody's neurons have the same capacity for doing so, but better learners use other types of strategies to retrieve information? The answers to these questions are unknown. It is known, however, that brain plasticity differs among individuals, especially in regard to recovery of function. For example, two patients with identical lesions in the brain resulting in language problems can have very different prognoses, with differences in the speed and degree of recovery of language six months later. It seems plausible that the neurons of some individuals are more plastic and therefore better at learning than those of a person with a lesser learning capacity.

Potential Problems

To realize the importance of memory, perform this simple experiment. Imagine for a moment that you have lost your memory. You are unable to recall who you are, your name, your past, your profession, your likes and dislikes. The people around you, many of whom you have known all your life, suddenly become strangers. You don't know their names, their relation to you, the way they are. Your house, your community, your room become strange places, as if you have never been in them before. If you lose your memory, in essence, you lose yourself.

In my years as a neurologist I have encountered many patients who have lost their memory. Some have done so for a few minutes or hours, other less fortunate ones for years or for the rest of their lives. Some patients are aware of their forgetfulness, others forget that they forget and are, therefore, unbothered by their inability to remember. The aware ones frequently undergo much suffering. I remember a particular patient, a 53-year-old university professor who lost his memory after suffering a viral infection in the brain. After a long and complicated hospital stay, during which he closely battled with death, he was discharged from the hospital. He went home with his wife and children, but a few months later he confided to me that on that day, he had gone to a strange house inhabited by strangers. That first night he shared a bed and was held by a woman he did not recall having ever met, although he had been married to her for almost 30 years. In the following weeks his loving wife and children tried their best to help him remember his past. He told me that his main emotion during those first months was of embarrassment accompanied by curiosity. He felt like an actor playing the part of himself as he was told he had once been. Strangely enough, he did remember his childhood and was shocked to learn of his parents' deaths several decades in the past. He grieved for their deaths as if it had just happened, as he had done many decades prior. Two years later when I saw him again, he had recovered some of his memory, but only to a small degree, and he was still learning about himself.

Amnesias

Amnesia refers to the loss of memory. The causes of amnesia are so varied that it would take an entire volume to discuss the topic thoroughly. Amnesia results from damage in many different areas of the brain, although damage to particular areas, such as the limbic and paralimbic areas, is more frequently associated with memory loss.

Traditionally, amnesia has been divided into two types: a disorder in the storage of memory, that is, in the laying down of new memories, and a disorder in the recruitment of pre-stored information. If we compare the storage and retrieval of information to the storage and retrieval of a product in a warehouse, we can understand this concept better. Let's suppose that a delivery of information is brought into the loading dock of the warehouse. A forklift operator picks up the information and stores it in a particular place, keeping a record of the storage site. When that particular information is needed, a message is relayed by the warehouse supervisor to a second forklift operator, who picks up the information and delivers it where it is needed. If the first operator becomes disabled, information cannot be stored; if the second operator becomes disabled, the stored information cannot be retrieved, although the storage of new information can continue. This example is a gross oversimplification, but it can help us understand certain disorders of memory.

Alcohol abuse, for example, can result in severe, well-defined disorders of memory. The most dramatic is called Korsakoff's syndrome. A patient affected by this condition is unable to lay down new memories and thus is incapable of learning new information, although he is able to remember things that happened long ago. Thus, the patient's storage of information is severely affected, although the retrieval is relatively spared. Confabulation is an important component of this disorder. A patient makes up information in order not to disagree with the person who interrogates him or her. For example, if a patient with this condition is asked whether the interrogator has seen him in the supermarket during the past week, the affected individual will answer affirmatively, even though this has clearly not been the case.

Patients with Korsakoff's syndrome will frequently seem unconcerned about their severe memory loss, probably because they are unaware of their deficits; that is, they forget that they forget.

Alzheimer's disease is another progressive condition in which memory, among other functions of the brain, is severely affected. Both the storage and retrieval of memory are affected. The cause of this devastating disorder is unknown, although many potential causes have been proposed.

5 Language

In the university where I work, I frequently train residents from foreign
countries. The resident interviews the patients and then discusses them
with me, then we examine the patient together. Since I stress to my students that an interview should always include questions about vocational
activities, one resident related that a particular patient was a sheep farmer.
I frequently begin a patient consultation with a joke or amusing comment
in an effort to put him or her at ease. Therefore, as soon as the patient and
his wife entered the examination room, I made the following comment:
"Before we begin, I would like to point out that in my country of origin, it
is customary for satisfied patients to reward physicians for their services
with products from their farm. I particularly enjoy the delicate flavor of
spring lamb." The patient and his wife looked at each other with a puzzled
look. After an embarrassing silence, the patient's wife timidly stated, "I'm
sorry, doctor, but we have no particular access to lamb." I directed an irate
look at the resident and told the patient, "I apologize for my comments,
but truly, I was only joking. The resident physician who evaluated you told
me you had sheep in your yard and I assumed you were a sheep pro-
ducer." Both the patient and his wife broke out laughing. "My husband
merely told him he worked in a shipyard," said the wife.

This story demonstrates the importance of words to human communication. In fact, what would you do without words? Think of the word *universe*. It encompasses the trees, raindrops, stars, animals, tears, winds, and
faces. Without the word, how would it be possible for a person to contain,

or "symbolize," such a complex thought as everything within the universe in the space occupied by a mere eight letters? Jewish mystics held that without the word *universe*, the universe itself could not exist. In fact, in Judaic tradition, the word precedes the actual universe in the act of creation. God first created the word, which actualized into the universe; and so with everything created. First the word, and then this same word, which contains within itself all the components of creation, "expands" to compose the creation. But what exactly are words? Are they merely symbols for objects or concepts? Let's explore this subject further.

ANATOMY OF WORDS

If we were to take a scalpel and dissect a word we would find that it is made up of one or more phonemes. *Phonemes* are the shortest units of sounds that can be uttered in a given language and that can be recognized as being distinct from other sounds in the language. Phonemes are thus the shortest units that can be emitted by the human mouth. The word *pat* has three phonemes: *pa*, *ah*, and *ta*. This word can be distinguished from the word *hat* because the latter has the phoneme *ha* as opposed to *pa*.

Each language has its own particular phonemes as well as ways of combining phonemes that help give the language its particular flavor. For example, you are able to detect someone next to you speaking French, even though you do not understand the meaning of the words, in part because certain phonemes in French are not present in English. (However, a number of other factors besides phonemes help us differentiate one language from another.) For example, the word *moi* in French has the phonemes *mo* and *a*, which are not present in this particular combination in English.

Phonemes help the brain separate and thus recognize words in a stream of words that are heard. The brain's ability to recognize individual words in spoken language is one of its the most fascinating abilities. Listen to someone speak. A speaking individual normally does not interject silent spaces between words, and yet the listening brain is able to recognize each individual word from the stream. The complexity of the task involved in segmenting the speech stream into meaningful language units is apparent when we listen to speech in a foreign language. It is impossible to tell where one word ends and the next begins.

And yet this is not a perfect mechanism. Look at the following examples of popularly misinterpreted statements quoted in part from the language scientist, Mondegreens:

A girl with colitis goes by. ("A girl with kaleidoscope eyes," from a Beatles song)

Our father wishart in heaven: Harold be they name lead us not into Penn Station. (Misinterpretation of the Lord's Prayer)

Gladly the cross-eyed bear. (Gladly the cross I'd bear.)

The stuffy nose can lead to problems. (The stuff he knows can lead to problems.)

The good candy came anyways. (The good can decay many ways.)

This ability to separate words from a stream holds true for verbal but not written language. You would have a hell of a time reading this book if all the words ran into each other with no spaces between them.

WORDS AND MEANING

The ultimate function of language is to convey meaning. In regard to language and communication, meaning is conveyed by a number of factors that we will discuss, but in regard to words, meaning is conveyed by both the reality for which the word stands, and very importantly, the way in which words are combined to relay a particular message. The process of combining individual words to convey meaning is called *syntax*.

Syntax is a tremendously important aspect of language. Examine the following sentences:

1. Boy ate cat.
2. Cat ate boy.

The exact same words are used in both sentences, but the difference in the order of the words makes a tremendous difference in the meaning. The syntax, or order in which words are used in a string, can also make that string meaningless. Examine the following sentence made famous by Noam Chomsky:

"Colorless green ideas sleep furiously."

This sentence has perfect syntax, or structure, that almost allows us to retrieve some kind of meaning from the words, but of course it is nonsense, given what we know about ideas and sleeping.

In any particular language, some words can stand by themselves and represent a particular reality (such as the word *cat*, which refers to an animal), but other words have no associated reality and are used only in the process of syntax to impart meaning to a string of words. These words, called *relational* words, include words such as *and*, *the*, *a*, and *with*. Newspaper headlines often lack "function" words and can thus be quite ambiguous, providing some evidence for the importance of these words in signaling important interpretive information regarding the relationship between words. Examples of these follow:

Hershey Bars Protest

NJ Judge to Rule on Nude Beach

Reagan Wins on Budget, But More Lies Ahead

We'll Have Harry for Dinner Tomorrow (how should we cook Harry?)

The power of syntax in providing meaning is enormous, but poor syntax can certainly contribute to ambiguity in our interpretation of language. For example, ambiguities of meaning arise when phrases are placed in a syntactic position that allow two possible interpretations. Let's look at the following examples corresponding to newspaper clippings:

For sale: Mixing bowl set designed to please a cook with round bottom for efficient beating.

Yoko Ono will talk about her husband John Lennon who was killed in an interview with Barbara Walters.

I know a man with a wooden leg named Smith. (We wonder, what is the name of his other leg?)

COMMUNICATION TOOLS

I recently attended an exhibition of native Eskimo art held in a local museum. The show included hundreds of masks. As I walked through the exhibition, it occurred to me that every conceivable human emotion was depicted by those masks. Motionless and without words, the masks conveyed anger, hate, rage, happiness, love, foolishness, and hope. If a static, unmovable mask can convey so much, think of the human face—an ever-changing mask, permanently communicating an infinite number of ever-changing messages.

Thus, communication and language involve much more than the meaning of words. When we convey a message, much of the meaning of that message is contained in our tone of voice, our facial expression, and our body movements. The exact same word spoken in an angry, sad, or happy tone of voice conveys a totally different message. The way we move our hands, faces, and the rest of our bodies also adds to the content of our messages. Think of a play in a theater. Who is the best actor? He or she who is best able to convey to the audience a particular message. A good actor is in fact a good communicator, one who utilizes his or her whole body to assume a personality and convey it to spectators, using his or her entire self to convey a message. The mere enunciation of words does not suffice.

Therefore, the content of a spoken message is contained in three modalities. The first consists of the factual meaning of the words that are spoken. The second component consists of what is known as *prosody*, which is the variations in pitch, amplitude, tempo, and rhythm that we utilize when we speak. A word spoken angrily contains a very different prosody than the same word spoken in a friendly fashion. Prosody can also help us understand sarcasm or irony contained in a sentence. The third component consists of the use of what is called *nonlinguistic codes*, that is, the body movements that we use when we communicate, including facial expressions, hand motions, and the like.

The meaning conveyed by a spoken message is thus the sum of these three components. With this knowledge, we can understand how a spoken sentence contains so much more meaning than the same written sentence and how a sentence spoken in front of another person contains more meaning than the same sentence conveyed over the phone. A written sentence contains only factual meaning; a sentence spoken over the phone conveys factual meaning plus prosody, and the sentence spoken face to face conveys all three (factual meaning, prosody, and body language). When we are face to face with somebody else, we can convey the most comprehensive message. Only in this situation are we able to detect incongruities among the factual message, prosody, and body language. E-mail, fax machines, or telecommunication can never replace face-to-face contact in the quality of communication.

In fact, we can also communicate without language, which is the way mimes convey messages. In some language disorders, such as Broca's aphasia (discussed later in this chapter), these nonlinguistic language cues are most of what the patient has left with which to communicate. Some patients do very well using these gestural and prosodic indicators to express their messages, never having to rely on language at all. It is believed that body language and prosody are "primal" and foundational aspects of language but somewhat independent of language itself (as we can see from these patients). That is, one can have communication without language, but not vice versa.

Words are therefore only one (although perhaps the most effective and efficient) of the tools that we use to communicate.

THE PURPOSE OF LANGUAGE

The most obvious purpose of language is that of communication. However, language serves a much broader purpose than communication. Language is one of the means (and probably the most eloquent) by which we store and organize information in our brain. As stated above, we contain objects, concepts, ideas, and experiences in words, which we then use to think, to manipulate information.

A question that has been asked many times during the centuries relates to the relationship between language and thought. The relationship between the way we think and the ways language is used to express thought is difficult to understand. Do we think with language? And if so, why is it that we frequently are unable to express our thoughts with words? Does a certain language predispose an individual or an entire culture to think in a specific way? These are very valid questions that have generated much discussion and little in the way of answers. Unfortunately, this topic merits much more discussion than we can devote to it here.

LANGUAGE DEVELOPMENT

Language as an Obligatory Human Function

Certain human activities are both universal and obligatory to the human race, regardless of culture or ethnicity. By universal, we mean that it is available to all humans with normal development, given our biological and genetic constitution. By obligatory, we mean that humans are genetically obligated to perform such activities. The reason for that obligatory and universal nature of those activities is that the mental "programming" for them is ingrained in the brains of all humans. Interaction with the environment is needed to bring those programs to realization, but learning of those activities comes in a natural and relatively easy manner. That is to say, it does not take much to teach or to learn to perform those activities. An obvious example of such "programmed" activity is walking. All humans with normal development and with appropriate stimulation learn to walk. In fact, most humans walk in a similar fashion, regardless of cultural differences or how well or badly they were taught to walk.

The same appears to be true for language. Certain areas of the brain contain the "program" for the acquisition and use of language. This program is universally contained in all humans, regardless of culture or language environment, and it appears to be quite an involved process, containing rules that are applicable to all languages. There clearly are numerous grammatical differences within languages, but these differences are believed to arise from surface features of the languages, such as the specific phonemes involved, and not in the underlying combinatorial rules that seem to be found across languages. In fact, concordances between languages by far surpass discordances. There are over 7,000 languages in the world, with enormous homogeneity in the way they express grammatical relationships. For example, 75 percent of the world's languages have a default sentence order of subject-verb-object, as in English.

Because of these ingrained programs, all humans acquire some type of language just by virtue of belonging to the human race. This genetic programming even directs the process necessary for the attainment of language. Thus, the sequential steps a child follows in the process of learning a language is similar for acquisition of all languages, regardless of culture. At one year of age, a child is able to utter and understand some words and perhaps some phrases (such as "Mommy gone"). At the age of three, the child is able to form full sentences, with only a few surface errors. By the age of four, a child's language structure approximates that of an adult. This is true for children across all specific language environments, although the specific language that the child will acquire will, of course, depend on environmental factors.

This preprogramming of the brain for language explains why children learn language, with its enormous grammatical complexity, in such a seemingly effortless fashion. A child masters one or even two languages before he or she is capable of solving simple problems in arithmetic, or before he or she can ride a bicycle. In fact, given the ease with which a child develops language, we have changed to the term *language acquisition* rather than *learning*. Much of the research on child development suggests that language is not learned in the traditional sense. This is shown by that fact that (1) children are resistant to correction, (2) children learn language even with relatively impoverished stimuli, (3) most children do not receive negative evidence (that is, parents generally do not overtly correct children when they are wrong), (4) children do not imitate (and often cannot imitate beyond their means), and (5) children create and manipulate words and morphemes in creative and generative ways that go far beyond the mere stimuli to which they have been exposed. The brain is set up to acquire language in such a particular way that the normal "learning" procedures (i.e., the ways in which we consciously teach other cognitive behaviors, such as the multiplication tables) are ineffective in a child's learning of language.

Does this mean that a child could potentially learn any language, regardless of the culture into which he or she is born? Apparently, yes, since the brain seems to contain the program for *all* the languages utilized in the world. Since it is possible for us to understand and learn another language, even as adults, it must be possible for us to have some biological mechanism in common by which we can interpret any of the world's languages. Some philosophers have suggested that there is or was a universal or primal language from which all languages stem; remember the story of the Tower of Babel in the Bible? In this narrative, all humans speak one language, but as punishment for building a tower to reach the sky, God creates different languages, with the result that people are no longer able to understand each other.

In fact, research has demonstrated that prior to learning a specific language, infants as young as 10 months are able to produce and distinguish a wide variety of sounds utilized in many of these languages. As the child learns a specific language, he or she loses the capacity to produce sounds that are not part of it. For example, Japanese infants are able to distinguish between phonemes that are not critical to word distinctions in Japanese, such as the *r* and the *l* phonemes. As the infant becomes older (about 13 months), he or she loses the ability to produce or distinguish between those sounds. It is the old "what you do not use you lose," phenomenon. It also seems to serve to pare down the amount of information the brain needs to store and retrieve. What is not critical information in a particular domain is no longer "perceivable" or "recognizable."

As a side comment, it is important to point out that the program the brain contains for language and that explains the ease by which language is acquired refers to verbal rather than other forms of language. Most humans learn to speak and understand auditory language independently of cultural or educational factors. We are yet to find a culture that does not have verbal language in some form, unless their hearing does not permit it (i.e., the deaf culture). The *manner* in which one speaks is certainly dependent on educational variables, but the *fact* that one speaks is not. Therefore, learning to speak and understand spoken language occurs earlier in a child's lifetime and with seemingly less effort than learning to read and write. Reading and writing involves declarative forms of learning to a larger degree than does learning of verbal language and probably involves sets of neural structures separate from those used in auditory language. Written language is also much more dependent on cultural and educational factors; a sizable amount of the world's population is, unfortunately, unable to read or write, and many of the world's cultures never developed the ability to do so.

TIME WINDOW FOR ACQUISITION OF LANGUAGE

We have learned that at certain well-delineated periods of time in an individual's life, frequently referred to as "time windows," the brain is most suited for the acquisition of certain skills. The acquisition of language is an excellent example of such selective plasticity. These time windows are universal, since all children, regardless of language environment, develop their language within specific time frames, or windows, that is, at similar time and age ranges. There is, to be sure, individual and within language variance in those time windows, but this variance is relatively small. The core or underlying features that all languages share, also termed *universal grammar*, is what appears to have a similar time course in acquisition. In the area of language acquisition research, one speaks of parameter variation of certain features that are "set" in the direction specified by the target grammar. For example, children speaking Japanese and those speaking English may set word order at roughly the same time in the course of acquisition, but Japanese children set the sentential order rule as subject-object-verb, whereas English-speaking children set it as subject-verb-object.

The importance of these time windows for language acquisition cannot be overstressed. Failure to take advantage of a time window for language acquisition can have drastic consequences. The first three years of a child's life are critical for the acquisition of language. The presence of certain traumatic circumstances, such as neglect or emotional or other types of abuse, during those critical periods of a child's life can have drastic and permanent consequences on the child's acquisition of language. Because most children are exposed to language in some form, there is relatively little information as to what happens to children not exposed to language in any form. As we have already said, even with the minimal amount of interaction with their parents, children learn language quickly and easily because the mind is preprogrammed to accept language stimuli. That means a young brain strives to make sense of the conversations of adults or older children, what they hear on the TV or radio, and other language they receive from relatives or friends, even if their parents neglect them. We also know that natural language can take many forms; it can be gestured (sign language), spoken, written, and even whistled (these languages have developed in the highlands of Turkey where other forms of language have been out-selected, given the long distance for communication). In any case, all of these factors make it difficult to test a case of development in the absence of any form of language whatsoever.

Unfortunately, such a case does exist. Her name is Genie, and she was about 13 when she was "discovered" by chance by a social worker. Genie was kept locked in a dark attic room by psychotic parents. She received no language stimuli except for occasional grunts, was severely undernourished, and was left in her own urine and excrement for days at a time. She had progressed through the important time window we understand for most of development. After being "rescued" from her situation, Genie learned to produce immature, pidgeon-like sentences such as "Mike paint" or "Applesauce buy store" but was permanently incapable of mastering the full grammar of English. Certainly, many social factors were involved in this case, going beyond the mere absence of language, and we cannot be sure to what extent her behavioral inability might in fact have been a result of brain damage due to the severe beatings she received on her skull. However, it seems that the acquisition of language after the lapse of the time window involves a very different learning process, one that requires much more effort in most language learners.

Within the critical time windows, children learn language through a nondeclarative process, without the conscious utilization of rules. As we discussed, this is a universal and obligatory process that requires a certain process that is not learned but "acquired" in the sense that it is not taught by parents. Instead, the underlying mechanisms of the brain that are pre-programmed interact with the language stimuli. A child asked why he says "I am" as opposed to "I are" will probably not be able to invoke the appropriate grammatical rule (my five-year-old niece answered with an angry "because" on being asked that question). Language is learned at that stage utilizing nondeclarative processes.

Most older children or adults, on the other hand, utilize some declarative processes to learn a language. That is, they must learn rules of pronunciation and grammar, apart from learning the meaning of words. Even if those rules are mastered, an adult will probably be less able than a child to achieve the extremely complex coordination of lips, tongue, and facial muscles necessary to perform perfect pronunciation of words. This failure to attain perfect pronunciation, which can be achieved only during the time of maximum plasticity, results in an accent. (As a native of a foreign country, I have more than ample experience in the matter. You, my dear reader, are unable to admire my prominent yet highly distinguished accent, because I talk but neither write nor think with it.) However, some learners of a second language do master native or near-native pronunciation skill. It is not clear to what extent nondeclarative processes might become involved at some point of second-language learning and to what extent individual language skills play a role in these differences in ability.

What about children exposed to more than one language? If this exposure occurs during the ideal time window for language acquisition, children are more likely to utilize only nondeclarative processes for learning the languages to which they are exposed. It has been difficult to separate nondeclarative from declarative learning, since most second languages are not taught in the same way as first languages. Teachers generally use declarative, explicit teaching methods to teach second languages and a second language is still usually taught through the first language, so it is not clear whether the second language could have been learned in a more nondeclarative manner, had it been taught differently. Amazingly, the brain can differentiate and correctly apply the appropriate grammatical rules for each of the learned languages.

The Yearning to Name

Humans have a built-in yearning or necessity to put a name on objects that they encounter, and on experiences that they experience. Because words are so powerful, naming, or encasing, reality into words becomes a fundamental human activity. In the Bible, Adam is asked to name all of the animals, as if by doing this he is assisting in and completing their creation.

This necessity to name is due to the fact that, as we discuss later, language is a way by which the brain organizes information. Thus, when a child encounters an object for the first time, he or she immediately wants to know what it is or what it is called. For example, upon encountering a horse, a child at once asks what the animal is. His peers will most likely answer, "That is a horse." As if wielding a magic wand, the child hearing this response will immediately contain the reality of the animal within the word *horse*. By naming the animal a horse, the child has incorporated the reality of the horse within himself. When the child hears the word *horse*, the image of the animal will immediately be recruited into his mind. The word and the object have become inseparable. The word *horse* will suddenly, almost by magic, cease to be a meaningless combination of letters. On the other hand, the horse itself will cease to be an unknown animal and will suddenly become a horse.

Yet naming is not a simple process. Consider the famous philosopher Quine's story, so often used to illustrate the problem and complexity of naming and thus of the acquisition of language. A man's plane crashes on a remote island whose inhabitants and language are unknown to him. He sees a rabbit hopping across the plain, and a native points to the rabbit and shouts "Gavagai!" How does the man know whether this word means *rabbit* and not *Unconnected pieces of rabbit parts* or *Rabbit ears* or *Running rabbit* or Notice the green grass behind the rabbit?

Children resolve this problem, at least in part, because the language program engrained in the brain contains a process for aiding the naming process. When we point to and label objects for children in the absence of a sentential context, we realize that children use certain default "rules" to determine meaning. However, it is the sentential context that helps "cue" the child the best as to the word's meaning. From the study of child language acquisition, there is some evidence that we seem to be preprogrammed to label objects or "name" events in particular ways. For example, Roger Brown showed children a picture of a person kneading a mass of squares in a bowl and asked, "Can you see any sibbing?" The children pointed to the hands. Although the word *sibbing* is nonexistent and thus the children had never heard the word before, the sound of the word led them to assume that it was referring to an action (such as *doing*). When he asked them, "Can you see a sib?" they pointed to the bowl. With the question "Can you see any sib?" they pointed to the squares inside the bowl. Many other studies have recently shown the ingenious ways children have of using sentence structure to understand individual word meaning.

In addition, some other studies by Ellen Markman have shown certain conceptual biases for labeling objects. When a pair of pewter tongs was called *biff,* the child interpreted this as meaning tongs in general so when asked for "More biffs," the child picked out plastic tongs. Then, when shown a pewter cup called *biff,* the child did not interpret this as *cup*, since the child knew cup means *cup*, so *biff* meant something else, and thus arrived at the stuff the cup is made of. Children seem to have other creative and clever ways of understanding when the whole or its parts or some feature of the whole is referred to. Most often, the syntactic context provides the greatest cues, but sometimes just knowing other labels and fitting all new items into a greater conceptual scheme works to help children understand the meaning of new words, as in the previous example.

In addition to preprogramming at the level of phonemic distinctions and lexical naming, evidence also supports the theory that we are preprogrammed to notice certain syntactic distinctions. Sound signals such as word-level stress appear to signal grammatical categories of words necessary for sentential interpretation, such as whether a word is a noun or a verb. In addition, recent research with infants shows that young, preverbal babies have preferences for those word orders most commonly produced in their culture's language. For example, Japanese babies prefer orders wherein the verb is found at the end, which is the order of their language, while English-speaking babies prefer to hear the verb in the second position—S-V-O—as it is commonly found in the target grammar.

WORD STORAGE IN THE BRAIN

Once an object has been named, a powerful *pairing* between the word and the named object occurs. Thereafter, under normal circumstances it becomes extremely difficult for the brain to separate the two. Can you think of the ocean without simultaneously thinking of the word *ocean*?

But what is the relationship in the brain between a word and the reality it stands for? Is the word stored in one area of the brain and the reality it stands for in another area, and if so, what is the connection between the two?

Further complicating the issue is the fact that language can take the form of several different modalities. There is the auditory and oral modality (that which is spoken [or sung or whistled] and heard), the visual modality (that which is written and read or gestured and seen), and some languages have been "translated" into the sensory modality (that which is felt, such as in Braille alphabets). Is there one single mental representation of the meaning of a word that can be accessed by any one of the forms? That is to say, is the mental concept of a dog stored in a specific area of the brain, and can that mental concept be accessed by the enunciation of a spoken word and/or the reading of a written word? Is there a link between the areas of the brain where the animal and the word are stored, so that when I think of one, the other instantly comes up in my mind?

Scientists have yet to come to an agreement on the answers to these questions. Some feel that there is a single storage site within the brain for a particular concept, object, or idea. This storage site contains all the information about the object. The storage site for the concept *lion* contains the smell, noise, visual representation, and everything else about the lion. The visual and auditory word *lion* are each stored in different areas of the brain, but they are connected with this storage site so that hearing or reading the word will recruit all the information contained in the lion storage site. Other scientists believe that specific characteristics of the lion, such as its smell, sound, and visual image, are all located in multiple interconnected areas of the brain. Visual or auditory contact with the word *lion* activates, due to multiple connections, all these different areas containing information about the lion.

In fact, as we will learn in the section on aphasias, certain lesions in the brain can interrupt this connection between a word and the object it represents. Thus, a person may hear the word *horse* and not know what it represents or may not be able to name a horse, despite the fact that he may know perfectly what a horse is when he sees one.

A second topic relevant to the storage of words in the brain is that of categorization. *Categorization* is one of the most important aspects of language, without which language would be infinite and therefore impossible. Categorization allows us to group objects with certain similarities or commonalties into language categories. All dogs in the world, small or large, aggressive or gentle, fall into the category *dogs*. What would happen if categorization was not a possibility? In a story by the Argentine writer Jorge Luis Borges, a young man loses the ability to categorize after he falls from a horse and strikes his head. He is therefore forced to name every individual thing in the universe. Since he is unable to place all dogs in the category dogs, he needs to put a different name to every single dog. This also applies for the same object he sees at a different moment in time. A dog he sees one moment receives a different name from the one he gives the same animal a few moments later. In an individual who is unable to categorize, naming becomes an infinite activity.

Words make up a mental lexicon in our brains. Many philosophers and linguists have argued about precisely how this lexicon is organized. How are words related to one another? Single words can elicit more than appear to be contained in the meaning and content of the word itself. That is, one word appears to be connected to other words we know that stand in certain meaning-relationships with one another. This is part of lexical organization, or categorization. But how exactly does this classification work? Perhaps words are classified by their meanings. If so, we could start with what might appear to be a simple distinction between living and nonliving.

If it moves of its own accord, is it living? Is a robot then considered living? Would you classify objects found in your home as furniture? How, then, can one categorize the rug or the telephone? As you can see, this process only becomes more and more difficult as we test it with more exemplars.

Some language researchers have abandoned the notion of trying to find "necessary and sufficient" features or even "prototypes" for categories. Instead, events, goals, emotions, and frequent context may determine categorization of words and their organization. For example, the word *Italy* evokes images of mountains, oceans, and villages, the smell of certain flowers and food, the sounds of waves and mandolins. The word *love* can evoke images and memories both beautiful and painful. Other words have different associations, some the same, some different, depending on who you ask. Even words that seem to be well defined, such as *prime number*, *uncle*, and *bachelors*, appear to have some qualities that make exemplars better or worse members of the category. We definitely have certain expectations that have nothing to do with the actual definition of words when we categorize. For example, children have a hard time understanding that a child younger than they, who does not bring them presents and wets his pants, could in fact be their uncle, given that the child is their father's brother.

LOCALIZATION OF LANGUAGE IN THE BRAIN

It is commonly stated that language is localized in the left side of the brain. If by that we refer to the localization of the mechanisms utilized for the expression and interpretation of the meaning of words in the context of syntactic expressions, that statement is to a large degree true. But we have learned that language also includes other components, including prosody, pragmatic context and inference, and paralinguistic codes.

The neuroanatomy of language, that is, the localization in the brain for differing components of language, is extremely complex, and new developments in our understanding of this subject are rapidly emerging. Most past studies that have localized language to any particular area of the brain did so by correlating a particular language deficit in a neurologically injured individual with a specific brain lesion evident on autopsy examination, or more recently, on radiographic brain imaging. Because damage to the brain tends to involve multiple areas, results of these studies are difficult to interpret. Newer studies, which promise to significantly change what we know about localization of language, are based on correlating the areas of the brain that become active on PET or other functional studies with a particular language function performed by a normal person.

A large problem with studying localization that still remains a serious challenge, even with the latest technology, involves the issue of mapping the brain into smaller units, which would allow us to pinpoint with precision where a certain area, corresponding to a particular function, is localized. Some researchers still use what are called the Tallarach coordinates, which are coordinates measured from a French woman's brain that are used as the reference point for the current brain. Others use Brodmann's areas, which are specified locations by a researcher named Brodmann, but those are still rather subjective. The problem with both of these methods is that brains appear to be almost as unique as fingerprints. So what might be a particular area in one brain may be up to 2 or 3 centimeters difference in another. A new technique using over 6,000 slices from 10 brains has come up with the most average brain. A complex computer program can convert the brain being tested, in the most objective way possible, to the coordinates of this "average" brain. Unfortunately, only very few researchers have the resources to be able to do these complex computations. The hope is that this will change as we continue to observe such widely disparate results from different laboratories in localizing the same behavioral activity.

All studies to date suggest that the areas of the brain around the Sylvian fissure in the left hemisphere make up a neural loop, involved in most aspects of the processing of auditory and oral language, that is, language that is heard and spoken (as opposed to that which is written and read). This holds true for most individuals; language localization in the right hemisphere is extremely rare. This loop is also involved in the gestural language utilized by deaf and mute individuals, suggesting that it is not only involved with oral but rather with the primary or main modality of language utilized by an individual. This loop incorporates areas in the frontal, parietal, and temporal lobes. Within this loop are three areas that have discrete functions related to language. At one end of the loop is *Broca's area*, located in the left frontal lobe. This area has been traditionally linked to language output, that is, to the production of language. At the other end of the loop is *Wernicke's area*, which is located in the left posterior superior temporal lobe and has been associated with the processing of incoming auditory language, that is, with the processing of the input of language. A third area, which appears to be diffusely located in different areas of the brain (even right hemisphere to some extent), is that which stores "concepts." In the case of the word *lion*, Wernicke's area contains the program for processing and understanding the word, Broca's area for the manufacture of the word, and the concept areas contain all the characteristics of the lion. Hearing or speaking the word connects Wernicke's and Broca's areas with the concept areas.

In fact, among all areas involved in language are a number of fibers, or connections, connecting all three. One such group of fibers is the arcuate fasciculus, which provides at least part of the connection between Wernicke's and Broca's areas. In the simplest of forms, this loop presumably works as follows: If a person is asked to repeat a sentence, the information reaches Wernicke's area, where it is processed so that the person understands its meaning. From there, the information travels through the arcuate fasciculus to Broca's area, where the mechanisms for speech production are located. The person is thus able to verbalize the sentence.

Although recent findings have disputed this language loop to some degree, it continues to be the leading theory that localizes language in the brain. As discussed next, damage at any level of this loop will interfere with the processing of language. In its simplest form, damage to Broca's area results in inability to produce language and to Wernicke's area inability to understand language. Damage to the arcuate fasciculus results in an inability to repeat what one hears. This is an oversimplification, but many clinical language disorders follow this pattern.

The mechanisms responsible for language prosody and paralinguistic codes appear to be localized in the right, rather than the left, hemisphere in most individuals, as discussed in prior sections on differences in the function between the right and left hemispheres.

SIGNS OF MALFUNCTION: APHASIA SYNDROMES

The inability to process some aspect of language, such as the inability to understand or express language as a result of brain damage, is called *aphasia*. The following classification of aphasia may be used as a general guide to identify symptom patterns; however, brain damage caused by a stroke, traumatic injury, or tumor rarely affects only one specialized area in the brain. Therefore, we must stress that clinically, these patterns are difficult to find as "pure" cases. As we have said, the terms Broca's and Wernicke's, although still prevalent clinically, are not used by language researchers, given their ambiguous reference to location. In addition, most clinicians do not detail deficits that affect only certain grammatical classes or only certain conceptual categories. This level of detail of investigation is usually determined only in research settings. Many of the standardized tests, such as the BDAE or the WAB, do not have the means to appropriately test for certain deficits. We often find different combinations of some of the features of these aphasias, such as a patient with good comprehension, neologistic speech, and apraxia.

Brocas Aphasia

The lesion site is on the frontal lobe of the dominant hemisphere, usually on the left side of the brain. The patient's ability to comprehend some types of auditory verbal information generally remains intact, but speech patterns are not fluent. Speech articulation is impaired, and the patient frequently has difficulty using grammatical structures. Usually these patients have difficulty determining the roles of "agent" and "patient" in complex syntactic structures such as reversible passives (e.g., "The man was washed by the woman"). The hardest phrase for such patients to say is something like, "No ifs, ands, or buts about it." That is, these patients often lack these functional morphemes in their output. These patients frequently are better able to produce and comprehend nouns rather than verbs, since verbs often contain the important information regarding thematic roles (e.g., agent, patient). Often, the patient exhibits apraxia, which indicates problems with planning and execution of the fine motor movements required for speech. The coordination of the facial muscles, lips, and tongue is poor for articulation, and thus the patient's verbal output overall may be significantly reduced in spontaneous communication efforts.

Transcortical Motor Aphasia

Transcortical motor aphasia is another nonfluent aphasia that rarely occurs. Again, auditory comprehension is functional, but verbal expression is significantly impaired. Speech may be agrammatical, and apraxic errors may be noted. The distinguishable feature of transcortical motor aphasics, however, is their surprising ability to repeat lengthy sentences, whereas a Broca's aphasic patient may repeat single words but not longer phrases or sentences.

Global Aphasia

Global aphasics demonstrate severely reduced language function for both receptive and expressive language skills. They have much difficulty with both auditory comprehension and verbal expression and have seriously limited functional communication overall. Facial expression, manual gestures, and vocal intonation (paralinguistic features of language) may, however, be preserved or developed with therapeutic intervention. Pragmatic communication skills are often still intact but difficult to assess given the language difficulties. For this reason, computerized language systems (e.g., C-VIC, Computerized Visual Communication) are often encouraged. Such patients provide evidence that humans can have "propositional" thought (required for communication), even in the absence of language.

Wernicke's Aphasia

The brain lesion site in Wernicke's aphasia is the posterior superior temporal lobe on the dominant hemisphere, which is generally the left hemisphere. Auditory comprehension for language is impaired. Jargon, nonsensical speech, and frequent neologisms (use of one word for another, e.g., "Cinderella went to the bank [ball]" or "He's so hungry [handsome]") characterize verbal expression. Sentence grammar appears somewhat intact, but morphological substitutions occur and sentence flow moves from one topic to the next. We are reminded of Chomsky's phrase, "Colorless green ideas sleep furiously," when listening to Wernicke's patients' their grammar appears intact, but meaning is lost. Conversational attempts with a Wernicke's patient are very challenging due to their poor listening and comprehension skills and ineffective verbal attempts to convey their intended message to the listener.

Conduction Aphasia

In conduction aphasia, the patient's auditory comprehension is functional and verbal expression is adequate, but the main deficit area is inability to repeat words. Occasionally, a patient's expressive language skills are reduced due to word retrieval difficulty and/or phonemic paraphasias (for example, the patient may say *dan* for *pan* or *dom* for *Tom*).

Anomic Aphasia

Anomic aphasia is primarily characterized by single word retrieval problems rather than sentence structural deficits during verbal expression. Patients struggle to find the words they desire to communicate their thoughts. They may use such words or phrases as *that thing, stuff,* or filler descriptive words in lieu of the target word. They may describe the word or talk around the word in an effort to relay their message. Fortunately, their auditory language comprehension and verbal fluency remain preserved. Verbal utterances are usually grammatically accurate. Communication with an anomic patient is achievable, given the listener's knowledge of the conversational topic or context.

6 Perception, Attention, Imagination, and Consciousness

Perhaps in no other area of neuroscience are we so perplexed with definitions as in the discussion of consciousness. For purpose of our discussion, we define *consciousness* as a mental state in which we are aware of events taking place within ourselves and our surroundings. This is by no means a perfect definition, but consciousness is one of those concepts that is difficult to elucidate, yet most of us know what it means to be conscious. The key word in the definition of consciousness is *awareness*. When we are conscious, we are aware of information from the universe external to ourselves and of our body, thoughts, and feelings.

Consciousness includes sleep, because when we sleep, we are aware of our dreams and, to a certain degree, our bodies and the world around us. This explains why nightmares, pain, loud noises, or other stimuli can awaken us. Thus, the only differences between wakefulness and sleep in respect to consciousness are the degree and the target of our awareness. An unconscious person and someone who is merely asleep may look the same to an onlooker, but the degree of brain activity of the two differs drastically, as we will discuss. Additionally, an unconscious person does not dream (which is a form of consciousness), nor is he or she amenable to being awakened by stimulation from within or outside themselves.

PERCEPTION

Perception is the acquisition, internalization, and interpretation by the conscious mind of a stimulus arising from outside or within ourselves. It is the process by which we bring information into our awareness. Our conscious interaction with the universe around us and with ourselves depends on our ability to *perceive* (or become aware of) both the circumstances that occur in the world around ourselves, that is, outside of our bodies, as well as what occurs within ourselves, including our perceptions of our bodies, our thoughts, and our feelings. Without perception, interaction with the universe inside or outside of ourselves would be impossible, since we would not be aware of such a universe.

In accordance with our definition, perception refers to the acquisition, internalization, and interpretation of information by the *conscious* mind, which means that perceived information needs to be brought *into the conscious realm*. Therefore, a prerequisite for perception is consciousness, since only when we are *conscious* are we aware of external and/or internal stimuli. A conscious state enables perception; in its absence, perception is not possible. An unconscious person lacks awareness of herself and the world around her, and thus is unable to perceive. Consciousness and perception are closely interrelated, but they are not the same thing. Consciousness is a *state of mind*, while perception is a *mechanism* for bringing (or *recruiting*) information into consciousness. True, perception requires consciousness, but consciousness can, in theory at least, be present in the absence of perception.

To be sure, a large amount of information originating from within and outside ourselves reaches the brain but never becomes conscious, but by definition, that information is not *perceived* because it does not enter into our conscious domain. That is to say, we do not become aware of it. The brain's recruitment of unperceived information guides much of our simple (such as reflexive) and more complex behavior, and it greatly exceeds the amount of information that we perceive. For example, we are able to walk because a large amount of information regarding balance, position in space, and the like is transmitted to our nervous system and processed without our awareness of it. This unconscious acquisition and processing of information is involved in basically all of human functions and is imperative for our survival. An amazing property of the human brain is its ability to process both conscious and unconscious information simultaneously and in parallel.

Perception and the Present

We are able to perceive only the present, since a stimulus needs to be present in order for us to perceive it. I can perceive a lion standing before me because I can see, hear, and smell him. If he moves to the side so that I can no longer see, hear, or smell him, I am no longer able to perceive him, even though the memory of that perception that occurred a few seconds ago (including the lion's looks, smell, and sound) can still remain in my consciousness. Similarly, once a fruit and its juices leave my mouth, I am no longer able to perceive its taste. In the absence of stimuli, we can only *remember*, but not *perceive*, their characteristics.

There are, however, some exceptions to this statement. An example is the brief persistent image that we maintain when we close our eyes after looking at bright light. A similar phenomenon occurs when we listen to loud sounds that suddenly cease, yet we continue to "hear" them for a brief moment.

But having said this, is it really the present that we perceive? As we will learn, the physiologic basis of perception is clear. Some sort of stimulus, a sound, sight, smell, taste, or feel, gets picked up by specific receptors that are part of the human body. The interaction between the stimulus and the receptor creates an electrical signal that is carried by nerve fibers to the brain. There is thus a *flow of information*. I smell a flower; the scent flows in the air from the flower itself to receptors within my nose. The receptors transduce this smell into electrical impulses. When these electrical impulses reach the cortex, they again are transduced into a conscious perception of what we call smell. All this involves the flow of information across some physical distance—from the flower to my nose, and from my nose a few centimeters to the olfactory cortex in the brain. Movement cannot take place in space alone; it must necessarily take place also in time.

Because this flow takes a certain amount of time, we can therefore argue that we can only perceive the past, since it takes time for the information to travel from the source to the primary cortex, where perception takes place. This is somewhat similar to gazing at a star, where due to the duration of travel of light, we see only the light that departed the star thousands of years ago. Because of our physiological makeup, we are therefore denied the perception of the present. Everything we perceive happened a few fractions of a second ago. All phenomenal perception is thus a perception of the past. However, perception of a stimulus that originates from outside ourselves is as near as we can come to perceiving the present. We cannot come any closer.

Categories of Perception

Perception can be viewed from a number of perspectives. First, it can be divided into *extrinsic* and *intrinsic* perception. Extrinsic perception consists of the perception of events that take place outside ourselves and in the universe around us. Intrinsic perception consists of the awareness of events occurring within ourselves, including the perception of our bodies, thoughts, memories, and feelings. At any one period in time, a person may simultaneously perceive both extrinsic and intrinsic occurrences; for example, while a person is driving, he or she could be aware of both the road in front and of his or her own thoughts and feelings. In reality, many neuroscientists do not include intrinsic perception within their definition of perception, assigning other terms to it, but I prefer to include it as one of the components in the process of perception.

Perception can also be divided into *phenomenal* and *nonphenomenal* perception. The former refers to the perception of information that can be gathered, expressed, or described through the senses, including images, sounds, smells, tastes, and touch. The latter is the perception of information that cannot be gathered nor described through the senses, such as the perception of thoughts and feelings. We neither see, hear, nor taste our thoughts or feelings. Extrinsic perception is always or almost always phenomenal, since what we perceive of the universe external to ourselves enters our awareness through our senses. We have no other manner of perceiving extrinsic information, as we will discuss. On the other hand, intrinsic perception can be either phenomenal or nonphenomenal. Intrinsic phenomenal perception refers to images, sounds, and, to a lesser degree, sensations of touch, taste, and smell that we generate internally, either by remembering or imagining them. Let's understand this better through an example. Suppose I ask you to close your eyes and imagine or remember the ocean. In your mind you could "see," "touch," or even "taste" the water. It would even be possible for you to "hear" the waves and "smell" the seaweed, all without having the ocean in front of you. As we will learn, certain areas of the brain are important for both extrinsic and intrinsic phenomenal perception. The mechanisms of the brain involved with extrinsic perception are much better understood than those for intrinsic perception.

Perception can furthermore be divided into *passive* and *active* perception. Active perception refers to the awareness of events we actively or voluntarily bring into consciousness. In the case of active extrinsic perception, we voluntarily choose to bring certain elements into consciousness by modifying our actions; for example, we look at what we want to see. In the case of active intrinsic perception, we have the capacity to voluntarily generate or bring into consciousness images, ideas, and events. Thus, as we discussed, if you close your eyes and wish to do so, you are able to visualize the ocean or listen to the song of birds or the sound of an orchestra. You are able to do so even though no such information is being carried to the cortex by eyes or the ears. Thus, your brain is able to generate stimuli, including thoughts, and visual and auditory imagery, *even in the absence of an external source*. Active intrinsic perception also includes *voluntary remembering*, that is, recruitment into consciousness of things or events that we have encountered in the past, as well as *imagination*, which includes bringing into consciousness events that we have not encountered previously. Active perception is also extremely important for the manipulation of information, as we will discuss.

In meditation, a person willfully directs his or her awareness toward a particular event or object. Most meditation techniques involve voluntary or active intrinsic awareness, that is, the voluntary steering of awareness toward a stimulus that willfully originates from inside ourselves, such as a thought or image. One of the main goals of meditation is to limit or at least control the degree of passive awareness.

On the other hand, passive awareness refers to the consciousness of objects or events that drift into consciousness without any active effort from ourselves. For example, memories or thoughts drift into consciousness spontaneously, with no effort on our part and frequently against our will. This differentiation between active and passive awareness is not just purely descriptive; there is much evidence that each type involves different areas and processes in the brain.

BRAIN MECHANISMS FOR PERCEPTION

Our bodies contain a sophisticated system dedicated to perception. In keeping with our definition of perception, structures are dedicated to the acquisition, internalization, and interpretation of stimuli. There are also mechanisms for selecting and filtering the information that we perceive. The components of this system include a number of structures both within and outside of the brain. These structures can be classified into four categories:

1. Structures responsible for the acquisition of information
2. Structures responsible for the transport of information from the source of the stimulus to areas of the brain responsible for the interpretation of information
3. Structures responsible for the interpretation of information
4. Structures responsible for limiting and selecting the information that reaches the areas in the brain dedicated to the interpretation of information

These categories are described in the following sections.

Structures for the Acquisition of Information

Our sense organs are the windows to the external world. Via our senses, we are able to capture sights, smells, taste, touch, and sounds. The types of sensation (vision, smell, sounds, taste, and somatosensory) are termed *modalities*. There are five modalities of information that humans can perceive: visual, auditory, gustatory, olfactory, and somatosensory. Other perceptive modalities that can be classified as a subset of the somatosensory include pain, position, temperature, and movement sensation. Each modality of information is captured by highly specialized cellular structures called *receptors*. Within one modality are different types of receptor that capture a specific characteristic of that modality. For example, the eye contains receptors for black-and-white information and other receptors for color.

Receptors have two functions. The first is to capture information, and the second is to transduce a the specific type of energy that they capture into electrochemical energy. Thus, the receptors for vision and hearing transduce light and auditory waves, respectively, into electrical impulses, which are then sent to the brain. All receptors, irrespective of the modality they captivate, change the information they obtain into electrical impulses. This is because, as we stated elsewhere, the brain can only manipulate electrical chemical information.

The fact that we have receptors for only five different modalities of information limits the amount of information that we can perceive to those five modalities. It is entirely possible that the universe around us contains other modalities of information that are banned to us, since we do not have the receptors to capture them nor the brain structures to process them. The Zohar, a book on ancient Jewish mysticism, talks about certain colors that exist but cannot be seen. The fact that we cannot perceive other modalities does not negate their existence. Let's imagine a remote island where a congenital disease destroys the hearing apparatus of all inhabitants. To them, sound does not exist, and it would be extremely difficult to convince them of its existence. This concept—that much may be occurring around us that we may not be aware of because of our inability to perceive it—has generated countless debates in the religious and literary spheres.

Are we able to capture extrinsic information outside of those modalities for which we have receptors? This is an extremely interesting and highly debatable question. We have all heard of persons having a sixth sense, by which we mean that individuals are able to perceive information outside of the five modalities, but what constitutes such sixth modality and sense is not clear.

To be sure, there are other perceptual modalities for which the "receptors" have not been clearly identified. For example, there is the perception of time, or of the passing of time, which is difficult to explain in terms of phenomenal or nonphenomenal perception. A person is able to state with a good degree of accuracy when a minute goes by or when an hour or day has elapsed. The perception of time is, as with all other modalities of perception, linked to consciousness. An unconscious person is not able to ascertain the time that he or she remained unconscious. Are there receptors for the modality of time?

Structures for Transport

The perception of extrinsic information implies an information flow, from the source of that information to areas of the brain where it is interpreted and processed.

First, there is flow from the source (in the case of the perfume emitted by a flower, the flower itself) to the receptors responsible for capturing that modality (in this case, olfactory receptors). After receptors capture a specific modality of information and transduce it into electrical impulses, these impulses need to be carried to the brain, where the information is processed and interpreted. The electrical impulses are carried by axons, which act in a similar fashion to wires transporting electricity over long distances. These axons and their cell bodies are compiled into nerves and tracts.

The pathway between receptors and the brain is not a direct route. Along the way are a number of "perceptual gatekeepers," which are brain structures with the indispensable function of filtering and selecting the information that is to reach the cortex. Without this system, perception would be impossible, since our brain would be flooded all times by the enormous amount of information constantly being captured by the sensory organs. One of the most important perceptual gatekeepers is the mechanism of attention.

Attention is the mechanism by which we concentrate or emphasize our perception upon a specific amount of information. A useful analogy is that of a periscope, which directs our vision toward a specific area of space. Without attention to select and limit the information captured by the perceptive mechanism, our brain would be overloaded to such a degree that it would make the interpretation and processing of that information difficult or impossible. Attention does not only pertain to perception; it pertains to all conscious mental processes. Thus, when we perform a certain task, attention allows us to direct our efforts (including our motor and cognitive abilities) to focus on performing only that task, without shifting our efforts to other activities.

Attention has both a qualitative and a quantitative element. The qualitative component, denominated the *attentional matrix*, dictates *what* we will attend to; the quantitative component, denominated *attentional tone*, dictates *how much*. Both components fluctuate from moment to moment, and neither component is ever absolute. That is to say, we cannot direct *all* of our attention to one single amount of information. No matter how much attention one devotes to perceiving a fragment of information, such as reading a book, loud noises or other stimuli in any modality will divert our attention, if only momentarily. This characteristic of attention is also imperative for our survival, since it allows us to perceive danger and other stimuli when we are attending to one task.

In our interactions, we are constantly shifting our attentional matrix and varying our attentional tone so that we can appropriately attend to a specific stimuli. Both the attentional matrix and tone are controlled by a number of mechanisms. Certainly volition plays a part; we can, to a significant degree, choose what event to attend to and how much to attend to that event. But other factors also play a significant role. As we stated, certain extrinsic and intrinsic stimuli intrude into our perceptive matrix without our control. That is the case with both phenomenal perception (such as noises and smells) and nonphenomenal perception (such as thoughts). Our volitional control over what and how much we perceive a specific stimulus is very limited.

But the nature of the stimulus itself can control the attentional tone and matrix. For example, the brain perceives changing stimuli more readily than it perceives constant or unchanging stimuli. Through a process called *habituation*, the most elementary form of learning, the brain will, within a matter of minutes, habituate, or "get used to" and cease to respond to a constant, unchanging perception, to such point that we will become unable to perceive it, as though it was not present. Such habituation occurs with smells, sounds, and all other modalities of information. A stimulus that is present constantly and with unchanging intensity will, in fact, become absent to our perceptive mechanism. Constant presence equates, in such cases, to absence.

Absolute habituation to a stimulus is rare because the intensity of a stimulus is rarely constant. For example, even though a sound may persist for a period of time with an unchanging intensity and pitch, even minute movements of our heads or changes in the conduction medium (such as slight changes in the wind) will vary the characteristics of the sound so that we will not habituate to it.

A second condition in which the intensity of the perception does not correspond to or varies with the intensity of the stimulus is called *sensitiza-*

tion, which again is a form of learning that involves the attentional mechanism. In sensitization, the brain learns to attend and react to a stimulus (usually a noxious stimulus) to which it has been exposed in the past with a greater intensity than it did before. This topic is expanded upon in the chapter on learning.

Structures for Information Filtering and Selection

As we discussed, most information about the external world that is captured by the sensory organs, such as the eyes and ears, is transduced into electrochemical impulses that are carried by nerves to the thalamus and from there to the cortex. The reason for this pause in the information pathway is that the thalamus acts as a relay station, an information censor, a gatekeeper that selects and allows only a portion of the information that it receives from the sense organs to continue on to the cortex. In fact, the amount of information that we hold in consciousness represents a fraction of the information carried from the senses to the thalamus. This control in the flow of information is a key process by which the brain controls the target and degree of awareness at any particular moment in time.

The purpose for the thalamus's censorship activity is that it would be impossible for you to be fully aware of the multitude of events that are taking place around you while you are involved in a particular task. Look around you. While you are diligently involved in reading this manual, much is happening around you. Music may be playing, family members may be making noise, sirens could be blowing outside, lights might be going on and off. If you were to attend to all of these events, you would be unable to focus on the reading, a serious mistake in my opinion as the author. Yet all of this information is reaching your senses, since you do not normally cover your ears when you read, nor do you wear blinders that limit your sight. Without the thalamus pruning the information from the senses, you would need to attend to all that is happening around and within you.

The thalamus's control over this information flow is overseen by a group of neurons called the nucleus reticularis thalami (commonly abbreviated NRT), which surrounds the main body of the thalamus almost like a mantle. The NRT's role is to inhibit the information flow at the level of the thalamus; that is, when a neuron in the thalamus receives a signal from the NRT, it will stop the transfer of the particular information it was about to transmit to the cortex.

How do the NRT determine which and how much of the information reaching the thalamus goes on to the cortex? Is the NRT an overzealous censor of information that acts on its own whims? The answer to this question is far from clear, but the NRT receives direction from two areas: the cortex itself and the ascending reticular activating system (commonly abbreviated ARAS).

The ARAS consists of a group of neurons located in the brainstem that send their connections to virtually all areas of the nervous system. Their purpose is to "awaken," or turn on, cortical neurons and therefore put them in a state of readiness to work. Interestingly, the "default" state of neurons is to be inactive, or "off." (One of my students remarked that this concept explained his permanent state of laziness and yearning for inactivity.) In the case of perception, the ARAS puts neurons in a state of readiness to receive perceptual information.

The ARAS itself also sends connections to the NRT. These connections transmit signals that inhibit the NRT's inhibition over other areas of the thalamus. This inhibition by the ARAS of the inhibition by the NRT results in the facilitation or allowance of information passing from the thalamus to the cortex.

The mechanism regulating attention not only consists of connections from the ARAS or NRT to the cortex. There are also connections in the opposite direction, that is, from the cortex to both the ARAS and the NRT. The purpose of these connections is to provide a mechanism by the which the cortex can direct the ARAS and NRT as to the relevance of the information received and thus instruct those centers to filter in or out information forwarded to the cortex. The cortex is more interested in new or changing stimuli than monotonous ones. For example, if a person is having a conversation while there is a monotonous sound in the background, such as music, the cortex will instruct the NRT to inhibit the transmission of that background information. However, if in the same situation there is a novel or new stimulus, such as a loud bang, the information will be transmitted to the cortex until it instructs the NRT to interrupt transmission.

In addition to being interested in *stimulus novelty*, the cortex will also instruct the NRT about information that it is particularly interested in, or the *behavioral relevance of stimuli*. Let's explore this issue with an example. If ambulances with their sirens on go by your house while you are reading this book, you may attend to the first set of sirens, because it is a novel stimulus. However, if sirens continue, you will soon stop paying attention to them. The reason is that the auditory cortex has instructed the NRT to stop transmitting the sound of sirens, since they are not really relevant to you. However, let's suppose that a person in the midst of robbing your house suddenly sees this manual, is captivated by its title page, and temporarily abandons the robbery proceedings in order to read it while sitting in your best couch with a glass of your best whiskey. If he or she hears sirens, he will immediately pay attention to them no matter how often they occur, because the sirens are relevant or important to him, considering he or she is in the middle of a robbery attempt.

This perceptual gating system is illustrated in Figure 6-1.

Mechanisms for Interpreting Perceived Information

Studies that have utilized PET scanning have strongly suggested that phenomenal extrinsic and intrinsic awareness takes place at the level of the primary cortex. This means that in order for us to be consciously aware of an image or an event, that is, in order for us to know that something is taking place within or outside ourselves, there must be activity at the level of the primary cortex. In prior chapters we discussed that the primary cortex is the cortical area, which is in direct contact with the senses. It is the one

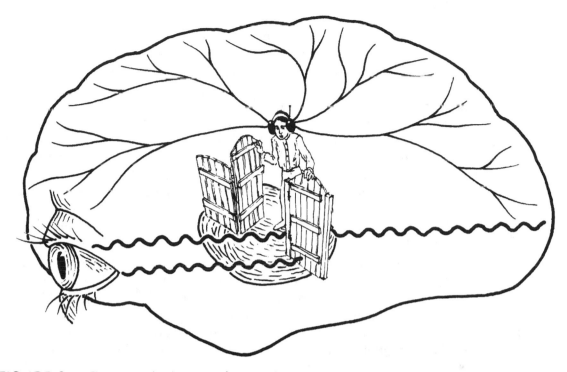

FIGURE 6-1   The perceptual gating system. A number of brain structures are responsible for selecting and filtering information captured by the senses before it reaches the cortex. The gating system does not act on its own. It also receives directions from the cortex as to the type of information to be allowed through.

area of the cortex that receives much (but not all) of the information carried from the senses. There is a primary cortex for each of the sensory modalities, including visual, auditory, sensory, olfactory, and gustatory. Therefore, the information regarding the subject of awareness must be carried from the source of the information (the senses) to the primary cortex corresponding to the modality of the information. For example, the awareness of visual information, such as occurs when we look at the ocean, necessitates activity at the level of the primary visual cortex. Similarly, awareness of auditory information, such as occurs when we listen to a song, involves activity of the primary auditory cortex. *Activation of the primary cortex is necessary for both intrinsic and extrinsic awareness.* For example, activation of the primary visual cortex occurs both when we look at the ocean (extrinsic awareness) and when we close our eyes and construct a mental image of the ocean in our minds (intrinsic awareness). This demonstrates that the primary cortex is just as important for the conscious awareness of extrinsic phenomena as it is for the awareness of internally generated or imagined stimuli.

But if the primary cortex becomes activated when we see the ocean or when we imagine it with our eyes closed, how does the brain know the difference? How does it differentiate between a real and an imagined stimulus?

This is a fascinating question that has been clarified somewhat in recent years by scientific studies utilizing PET imaging. As we discussed, these studies have suggested that the areas of the brain that become activated when we become aware of phenomenal events correspond to the modality of the information of which a person becomes aware. This is true whether the event being consciously perceived is intrinsically or extrinsically generated. So, how does the brain know if the image is externally or internally generated? That is, if a person is listening to a symphony or humming the symphony in her mind, and the auditory cortex becomes activated in both situations, how does her brain know whether the symphony is real or imagined? The answer is far from clear, but PET scan studies have shown that when the stimulus is intrinsically generated, the frontal lobes also become activated, which does not occur in the case of extrinsically generated stimulus. This finding points out that the frontal lobes possibly have an important role in the internal generation of stimuli, as well as in the conscious differentiation of real or imagined stimuli.

The ability to differentiate between information that arises from outside ourselves and that which originates from within ourselves (such as thoughts and internally generated images) is fundamental for our perception of reality and thus for mental health. Indeed, difficulty, in making this differentiation is one of the hallmarks of severe psychiatric disorders. For example, patients with schizophrenia may interpret their own thoughts as coming from outside themselves, frequently taking the form of voices commenting on or directing their behavior. Recent research suggests that some schizophrenic patients may have abnormalities in the frontal lobe or in its connections with other areas of the brain. Since the frontal lobe seems to be vital in the differentiation between real and imaginary perceptions, schizophrenic patients may mistakenly interpret internally generated stimuli as coming from outside themselves. This could at least explain in part why patients with schizophrenia suffer from *hallucinations*, which are the perception of sounds (frequently voices) or images with no actual source.

The importance of the primary cortex in the awareness of both extrinsic and intrinsic awareness is evidenced by the phenomenon called *blindsight*, which is most often found in patients who suffer strokes that damage the entire visual primary cortex. Patients with this condition are able to perform complex behaviors in response to visual stimuli, including colors and the like, but they deny that they are able to see the stimulation to which they are responding. This is clearly an example of behavior that is driven by an unconscious perception and processing of information. The phenomenon of blindsight provides significant proof to the postulate that there is a realm of behavior that can often be not just reflexive but in fact very complex and that is driven by unconscious processes. This proof could possibly indirectly support some aspects of the psychoanalytic theory.

THE INDIVIDUALITY OF PERCEPTION

Our perceptive mechanism is not a mirror. A mirror merely makes a two-dimensional replica of an object placed in front of it. The end product is merely a reflection, and the mirror neither adds to nor detracts from the image. With very minor differences, all mirrors in the world create the same image upon reflecting the same object. Additionally, a mirror does not maintain a memory of past images with which to influence its reflection of future objects. It reflects every image with no preconceptions, as though it were doing so for the very first time, even if the mirror has been exposed to that image in the past. A mirror, therefore, is immutable. It is not modified in any way by the images it reflects.

Unlike a mirror, our perceptive mechanism creates a *mental representation* of what is placed before it. This mental representation results from the *interaction* between the object perceived and our perceptive mechanism. The mental representation is dependent upon both characteristics of the perceived image and characteristics of the perceptive mechanism.

An analogy that can help us explore this complex concept is to view the perceived object as a seed and the perceptive mechanism as the soil in which the seed is planted. The mental representation is an "instantaneous plant" that results from interaction between seed and soil. The quality of the plant is dependent on the quality of both the seed and the soil. The character of the plant that grows from that interaction between seed and soil is a reflection of both.

This comparison between seed and soil and object perceived and perception mechanism can, at first sight, appear to be something of a peculiar analogy, but it helps us understand the manner by which the brain perceives the universe outside and within ourselves. The soil that is about to receive the seed is not a static structure. It constantly changes, and most important, it is amenable to change. It can be made more or less fertile, more or less moist, more or less receptive to the seed, all factors that will affect, to large degree, the quality of the plant that is to grow from the planting.

The uniqueness of an individual's perception of reality lies in the fact that each individual contains a different "soil," uniquely shaped by his or her prior experiences and exposures, including the efforts devoted to "fertilizing" such soil. In the presence of the same external stimuli, the mental representation created is unique to each individual.

In fact, one of the characteristics of the perceptive cortex is its plasticity, its ability to change with prior experiences. As we discussed, recent research suggests that the brain is a far cry from the static structure that it was believed to be only a few decades back. In fact, the brain is a structure that is constantly changing both structurally and functionally, constantly adapting to the demands placed on it by the reality external and internal to it. This ability to change its function and structure is appropriately deemed *brain plasticity*.

Although this holds true for all brain functions, it is especially pertinent to the perceptive apparatus. The structural and functional characteristics of brain cells are both the effect and cause of human activity. In terms of perception, the perception of an object may change our brain in such a way that future encounters with that same object can result in a different perception of that object, depending on the experience that we have accumulated with each particular perception. It is as though a reflection changes a mirror's manner of reflecting future reflections. There are no "casual" encounters with the world around us. Whatever we interact with in our daily living changes us forever. For example, reading this book will (hopefully) change the way you perceive everything related to the brain.

The number of factors that shape our perceptive apparatus are multiple, but they certainly include prior experiences with the perceived object, learning, and prevailing mood. Life experiences are the fertilizer with which we cultivate that soil. A straightforward illustration of this concept is learning the meaning of a word that was previously not known. For example, in Spanish, the word *leon* means *lion*. From now on, your encounter with the word *leon* will bring up an image of a lion. Your perception of the "seed" word has now changed. A permanent change has resulted in the "soil" of your perceptive apparatus.

Learning is, in fact, one of the most important voluntary tools for shaping a perception. Learning about music, for example, will change the mental representation a person makes when she or her hears a tune. Learning includes the incorporation of social norms, moral codes, and so on. A society that perceives murder as acceptable perceives murder very differently from a society that does not.

This brain plasticity as it pertains to perception provides us with a unique opportunity to enrich our perception of reality. The ability to cultivate the perceptive mechanism to guide the mental representation of a perceived object is humanity's greatest ability to rule, to a certain degree, the circumstances and universe around and within us. This cultivation of the perceptive mechanism in a positive direction can lead to a richer, more meaningful perception of the universe outside and within us. Even if reality cannot always be changed, the mental representation that a person makes of that reality can certainly be influenced in a positive manner.

IMAGINATION

Imagine. How many times have you used and heard that word? Have you ever paused to attempt to define what it means? I, who as I am sure you, dear reader, have figured out by now, clearly have little else to do in life, have given the matter a considerable amount of thought. In reality, I have always been fascinated by this unique human capability that enables us to dance, travel, sing, suffer—in sum, live almost every possible experience, albeit in a limited fashion, without moving a finger. All of this occurs in the relative safety of our minds. But imagination has a much more important role than allowing us to escape a boring class by daydreaming that we are Superman, or Macho Man, or Amazing Woman, or even Supersonic Toaster. Imagination is a critical activity for brain development and for successful everyday living.

How do we define imagination? There are many ways, but we will define it as the conscious manipulation of phenomenal information. As we discussed, phenomenal information is that which can be captured or described through the senses. It includes visual, auditory, gustatory, olfactory, and sensory data. In imagination, we mostly manipulate visual and auditory information, although other modalities can also be imagined.

Imagination is a theatrical stage on which we are able to write the script, design the set, select the actors (frequently unselfishly giving the most important roles to ourselves), and sit back to direct and observe the performance. On this theatrical stage, we incorporate information that we have encountered in the past and combine it with circumstances that may have never occurred before. I can imagine myself walking on the beach hand in hand with a person with whom I am infatuated. Both the beach and the person may have been encountered in the past in some fashion, but my imagination puts them together in a wishful circumstance never before encountered. Memory is thus an integral part of imagination.

What is the relationship between imagination and thinking? They are closely interrelated, but in thinking we manipulate ideas, and in imagination we manipulate phenomenal information, most notably visual and auditory data, although other sense modalities can also be imagined. There also appears to be an important difference between imagination and thinking in terms of functional brain activity. In imagination we utilize our primary sensory cortex, while in thinking with nonphenomenal information the primary cortex is less active. We discuss this subject in more detail in other sections.

Why is imagination so important? First, it allows us to try out alternative solutions to problems in our minds, as opposed to performing them in real life. Thus we are able to foresee possible consequences of each potential solution. That is, when we plan a certain activity, we can imagine alternative ways of performing it before we perform it in real life. This ability, which in essence is foreseeing potential consequences of our behavior, prevents us from making more mistakes in real life. In essence, this practice equates to foreseeing the future.

Second, imagination is important for creativity because it allows us to create a mental representation of a finished product before we begin the act of creation or while we are in the process of its completion. It is, in essence, the first step in creativity, the visualization of the finished product. The ability to imagine alternatives is probably one of the factors that most contributes to changes in the human race.

Imagination also has an important role in brain plasticity, one that has yet to be fully explored. Recent studies have shown that athletes who visualize in their minds movements that are required in the performance of a sport (in essence, imagining) show notable improvement in the real-life performance of those movements. This suggests that imagination has a fundamental role in learning motor and cognitive activities. Imagination is thus a critical activity for brain development. Additionally, imagination could have a fundamental role in the recovery of patients who have suffered neurological injury. It is conceivable that patients' visualization of movements that have been lost could lead to actual improvement in the performance of those movements. Some preliminary research data shows that this indeed could be so, but the matter needs further investigation.

What is the relationship between imagination and dreaming? Some see dreaming as the epitome of imagination, or imagination without restrictions. For example, the thirteenth-century philosopher Averroes thought that dreaming was the ultimate form of imagination. There are, in fact, significant similarities between dreaming and imagination. For example, both involve the use of similar phenomenal activity, mainly visual and auditory imaging. It is also conceivable that dreaming and imagination may serve similar purposes. In the section on sleep, we discuss theories suggesting that dreaming may provide a stage on which we are allowed to rehearse activities that we may be required to perform in real life. Imagination may have a similar function. However, imagination involves volition, while dreaming is presumably involuntary.

Is imagination an activity unique to humans? This is an extremely difficult question to answer. It is very likely that of all the animals, humans have the greatest capacity for imagination. Certainly creativity, which is highly linked to imagination, has its greatest expression in humans. Animals have a limited ability to create new things. For example, ants are able to construct incredibly sophisticated anthills, but those anthills are pretty much the same as those constructed by thousands of generations of ants before them. This does not hold true for humans. Each generation devises new ways of solving problems than the generations that come before.

THE FRONTAL LOBE AND ACTIVE AWARENESS

The frontal lobe has an important function in intrinsic active awareness, that is, the voluntary recruitment of material into consciousness. It has a decisive role in both imagination and remembering.

Active awareness is extremely important for the conscious manipulation of information. All behavior that is not reflexive involves the manipulation of information. For example, a person who needs to get from point A to point B needs to decide whether to go or not, evaluate all possible options, decide on a road to take, and modify the road taken according to situations he or she encounters along the way. All of these activities, including planning, initiation, evaluating all possible options, deciding upon a course, and modifying the course according to feedback, are frequently referred to as *executive functions* of the brain and represent the highest degree of human cognition. Executive functions require the conscious manipulation of information, that is, information must be kept in mind to develop a plan. Executive functions clearly involve activity of the frontal lobe.

It follows that the frontal lobe has a decisive role in one of the most unique and most elevated of human qualities: the capacity to create. Creativity involves the conscious manipulation of information to come up with the created substance, whether an idea or a concrete object. Creativity is related to, although very different from, problem solving.

BRAIN MECHANISMS RESPONSIBLE FOR CONSCIOUSNESS

The brain structures responsible for maintaining consciousness overlap those responsible for attention. As we discussed, in order for us to be conscious or aware of our surroundings and events taking place within ourselves, two processes must take place. First, information regarding the subject of awareness must reach the primary cortex, which implies a flow of information from its source to neurons in the cortex. Second, those cortical neurons to which the information is being sent must be ready to receive the information, which means that they must be "on." The brain's control over the degree and the target of awareness rests in its ability to control these two processes.

Multiple areas of the brain contribute in some way to the maintenance of consciousness, but two areas have a fundamental role: the first, the ARAS plays a prominent part in both "turning on" neurons and in regulating the flow of information; the second area, the NRT, has a prominent role in the regulation of the flow of information from its source to the cortex. It must be understood that this statement is an oversimplification, since both the ARAS and the NRT have some role in both turning on neurons and the flow of information.

As we discussed, the ARAS consists of a large group of neurons located in the brainstem. These neurons send connections to the thalamus (primarily the NRT) and to multiple areas of the cortex. When a cortical neuron receives a signal from the ARAS, it results in it being turned on. As we discussed, the "default" status of cortical neurons is off, and only when activated by the ARAS do they become turned on. The ARAS does not regulate consciousness on its own. It itself receives connections and direction from multiple areas of the brain, including the peripheral nervous system, cortex, basal ganglia, and cerebellum. This indicates that multiple brain sites participate in assisting the ARAS in its maintenance of consciousness. For example, the connections between the peripheral nervous system and the ARAS cause us to wake up when somebody pinches us when we're asleep. Other connections may explain why we wake up during certain dreams. Because the ARAS is as active during wakefulness as during REM sleep, some neuroscientists have argued that REM sleep is characterized by intense attentiveness to internal rather than external stimuli.

SIGNS OF MALFUNCTION: DISORDERS OF ATTENTION AND CONSCIOUSNESS

Coma

From the absolute extremes of total unconsciousness to normal awareness lies a wide spectrum of degrees of consciousness. The extremes of this spectrum, which include normal consciousness and coma, are easier to describe than the other conditions that lie somewhere between these two extremes.

At one end of the spectrum is *coma*. A comatose patient is totally unaware of his or her surroundings and, we presume, of his and her own thoughts and other components of his or her internal world. Thus, both extrinsic and intrinsic awareness are affected. A comatose patient is very different from one who is asleep. In sleep extrinsic awareness is limited but not abolished, since strong stimulation in all modalities (such as bright lights, loud noises, strong smells, and sensory stimulation) can awaken a person. Intrinsic awareness is similarly decreased but not abolished, which explains why we wake up during especially emotionally charged dreams. Additionally, intrinsic awareness, especially the awareness of dreams, persists during sleep.

Coma can result from a number of conditions, including head injury, strokes, infections, and other metabolic abnormalities such as severe kidney or liver disease. Although perhaps an oversimplification, it is helpful to understand coma as damage to the areas of the brain responsible for consciousness.

Therefore, damage to the ARAS results in coma because the system (the switch) responsible for turning cortical neurons on is damaged. We discussed that the "default" state for neurons is off. Only upon receipt of signals from the ARAS do they turn on. In the absence of such signals, they remain off, unable to receive, process, or act upon information forwarded to them. Large lesions in the brainstem, where the ARAS is located, therefore frequently result in coma. Traumatic brain injuries as well as hemorrhages and strokes that involve the brainstem are frequent culprits.

Damage to a large volume of the cortex also results in coma because the neurons responsible for receiving, processing, and acting upon information are damaged, even if the ARAS and other areas responsible for turning on neurons and for the flow of information to the cortex are intact.

Damage to the entire cortex can result from very large strokes, hemorrhages, and brain tumors. Damage to the cortex, both temporary and permanent, can also result from metabolic abnormalities, including irregularities in blood glucose and electrolytes. Overdose of drugs or alcohol also has the potential to damage cortical neurons in such a way as to result in coma. Severe endocrine, liver, and kidney disease, to name a few causes, results in metabolic abnormalities that affect the function of neurons and also result in coma.

Between the colors of black and white is wide gamma of shades of gray, which are difficult to name. Similarly, between the two extremes of coma and normal awareness lies an entire gamma of degrees of consciousness that are difficult to classify. Terms such as stupor, clouding of consciousness, and delirium are used by clinicians but have little intrinsic meaning.

Why do patients recover from coma? We have discussed that coma can result from damage to the ARAS or to large areas of the cortex. Damage can be temporary, such as that which occurs when a boxer is struck in the head, loses consciousness, but recovers fully within a short period of time. Loss of consciousness in this case results from temporary but reversible damage to the ARAS caused by the blow. In other cases, areas of the ARAS or the cortex may be more seriously damaged. Severe damage results in irreversible coma, but less acute damage to the brain can result in recovery of the functions of the areas responsible for consciousness.

We discussed that awareness has both a qualitative and a quantitative component. Patients emerging or recovering from coma go through a number of stages in which there are varying degrees of recovery of each component. For example, a patient's degree of awareness may recover but he may be unable to channel that awareness to a particular task. This can result in the patient's decreased ability to pay attention and easy distractibility. This inability to direct awareness may thus result in the inability to filter out stimuli, which presumably results in excessive information reaching the cortex and thus resulting in confusion or even delirium. With recovery, there is a progressive increase in the quantitative aspect of awareness and an improved capacity to utilize attentional mechanisms to target awareness to specific events. Interestingly, certain aspects of awareness may recover in patients who appear unresponsive. Many patients who emerge from coma are able to recall conversations held by people who were around them while the patients were comatose.

Further adding to the patient's confusion is the fact that emergence from coma is frequently accompanied by a patient's inability to differentiate between an imagined or a real stimulus.

Neglect

One of the most fascinating and perplexing conditions in neurology is that of *neglect*. The brain appears to divide awareness of the universe into two sides (left and right), divided by a vertical line. A patient suffering from neglect fails to attend to or act upon either the left side or the right side of the universe in front of him or her. In its most severe form, a patient afflicted with neglect behaves as though one side of the universe suddenly ceased to exist. A patient afflicted with left neglect. for example, may deny that his left hand or leg belongs to him. He may totally ignore events that take place on the left side, as though they were not occurring. He will not see or hear objects placed on his left side. When reading, he will read only words on the right side of the page and will write only on that side. Interestingly, neglect does not involve only objects that occur externally to an individual. In a fascinating experiment, Italian patients with left-sided neglect were asked to describe from memory Saint Mark's Square, a highly popular site in Rome. The patients described only the right side of the square, as though the left side did not exist. Thus, neglect has a motor component (failure to act upon one side), a perceptual component (failure to perceive one side), and an ideational component (failure to make mental representation of one or the other side).

Theories about neglect abound, but many researchers have suggested that it may result from the interruption of ARAS fibers going from the brainstem or the thalamus to the cortex. Since the ARAS is responsible for turning on cells in the cortex, interruption of those fibers results in the cells assuming their default, which is off. Therefore, information will not reach the cortex or will find the cortical cells turned off, which will result in the clinical manifestations of neglect.

Neglect is most often found in patients with lesions in the right parietal lobes, thus taking the form of left-sided neglect. Right-sided neglect is less common, but the reasons for that are not totally clear.

7 Sleep and Dreaming

The Body at Rest, The Brain at Work

We sleep one-fourth to one-third of our lives, and we dream for more than one-tenth of our lifetimes. Yet most of what we know about sleeping has been discovered only in recent years.

WHAT IS SLEEP?

For many years it was thought that sleep was a negative phenomenon, and the brain turned itself off during sleep. Today we know that this is far from the truth; in fact, the brain consumes more oxygen and glucose during certain stages of sleep than during wakefulness. This indicates that the brain is as or more active during sleep than when a person is awake, but the type of activity is different in each stage. It can be said, nonetheless, that during sleep the brain turns off *conscious* activity so as to concentrate fully on *nonconscious* processes. Even in the deepest stages of sleep, however, the brain is far from disconnected from the environment, since it continues to receive information from all of the senses and to send information to the rest of the body. Therefore, while your body rests during sleep, your brain actually works harder, and the type of work it performs is indispensable for survival. The reason you become tired at night is not because your brain requires repose, but because it needs to perform certain activities that it can carry out only during sleep.

STAGES OF SLEEP

Much of what we know about sleep has been discovered by exploring the electrical activity of the brain in sleeping individuals by means of a device called an *electroencephalogram*. Two stages of sleep can be identified. During the first stage, called *slow-wave sleep*, high-voltage but low-frequency electrical waves are recorded from the brain. Throughout the second stage, low-voltage but high-frequency waves are detected. Also during this second stage, the eyes move very rapidly in all directions, giving this stage its name, *rapid eye movement*, or *REM, sleep*.

REM sleep appears to be produced and regulated at least in part by a certain group of neurons in the brainstem that transmit electrical impulses (called *pontino-geniculate-occipital spikes*) during this stage of sleep to numerous areas of the brain, including the thalamus and the visual and auditory cortices. These electrical spikes are responsible for eye movements and possibly for dreaming during REM sleep.

Most individuals awakened during REM but not during slow-wave sleep report dreaming, which suggests that dreaming is the main mental activity taking place during this stage. Additionally, most muscles in the body (except the heart, eye muscles, and muscles involved in breathing) become paralyzed during REM sleep. This paralysis occurs, presumably, so that a person does not act out his or her dreams. In contrast, active body movements continue during slow-wave sleep. Sleeping individuals in this stage make a major change in their position every 20 minutes, and many do so more frequently.

During the REM stage of sleep, the body loses the ability to regulate its temperature, which becomes the same as the ambient temperature. Therefore, a person stranded in cold temperatures who falls asleep and goes into the REM stage is at risk of freezing to death. REM sleep is also the stage of sleep in which the brain is less responsive to external stimuli. A person in this stage is less likely to be awakened by noises or lights from the environment. However, a person is more likely to awaken spontaneously (without a clear cause) from REM sleep than from slow-wave sleep. In males, erection of the penis occurs virtually every time a sleeper goes into REM sleep and is unrelated to the content of a dream. The significance of this occurrence is unknown. In contrast, movement of the eyes occurring in REM sleep appears to be correlated with the content of dreams; emotionally charged dreams are associated with more frequent eye movements than uneventful dreams. Some investigators have suggested that the eyes "scan" or "look" at the dream during sleep.

During a typical night of sleep, an adult alternates between short periods of REM and longer-lasting periods of slow-wave sleep, each stage recurring from four to six times. The REM periods are longer in the latter part of sleep. Thus, sleeping individuals are more likely to dream closer to the time they wake up in the morning than when they initially go to sleep. REM sleep accounts for approximately 25 percent of total sleep time in young adults, but it represents 50 percent of sleep time in newborn babies, who tend to sleep approximately 16 hours a day. Interestingly, the need for REM sleep begins while a baby is still in the womb. REM sleep accounts for

80 percent of total sleep time for premature infants (Are those infants dreaming?). After birth, the need for REM sleep decreases and stabilizes at 25 percent by age 10—the same amount required by adults. REM sleep decreases significantly after age 60. In summary, infants and children not only sleep more, but the percentage of REM during their sleep is also greater than in adults, which means they spend much more time dreaming.

DREAMING

What are dreams? There is much we do not know about dreaming, but there is a lot we do know. First, all mammals and birds, with the exception of the spiny anteater, dream. In contrast, snakes and other reptiles do not dream. This fact provides an interesting insight into the relationship between dreaming and evolution of species. The spiny anteater is a *monotreme*, or egg-laying mammal. Monotremes were the first mammals to develop from reptiles. Marsupials and placentals diverged from monotremes approximately 140 millions of years ago, which suggests that REM sleep originated at that time. Thus, dreaming is a characteristic of more advanced species in the evolutionary scale.

Who dreams? Every human dreams; in fact, we dream approximately four to six times during a night and probably at all other times we sleep for any significant amount of time. Some people think they do not dream, but they simply do not remember their dreams. In fact, whether one can or cannot recall dreams depends solely on the phase of the sleep cycle in which one awakens. Most people who wake up during the REM or dreaming stage of sleep remember the content of their dreams. A person who sleeps undisturbed for the whole night is most likely to remember only morning dreams, the last dream that he or she dreamt. As we mentioned before, a person dreams more in the latest stage of sleep than in the earliest. Interestingly, dreams occurring later in the sleep period are longer, have more visual intensity, and are more emotionally charged than those occurring early in the night. Thus, most nightmares or terrifying dreams occur late in the sleep cycle, in the hours close to the time of waking up.

The Purpose of Dreaming

Why do babies and infants devote so much more time to dreaming? Why do the elderly dream less than young adults? In short, why do we dream? This question has occupied humans for thousands of years, yet the answer remains, to a large degree, a mystery. In the Bible, many of the prophets obtained the content of their prophecy during a dreaming stage, and thus dreams were the source of communication between God and man. In numerous cultures, dreams are predictors of future events, although the meaning of a dream is frequently expressed in some secret manner that requires an interpreter. That is the case in the story of Joseph and the Pharaoh in the Bible. "As long as a dream is not interpreted, it is like a letter that has not been read," says Rabbi Hisda in the Talmud.

Interestingly, the importance given to dream interpretation is exemplified in the Talmud by the belief that the manner in which a dream is fulfilled is dependent on its interpretation. Thus, R. Banaah tells how in Jerusalem there were 24 interpreters of dreams. Once he dreamed a dream and consulted with all of them. Even though not one agreed with another in the interpretation of the dream, all the interpretations were fulfilled, confirming the saying, "All dreams follow the utterances of the mouth." In a similar vein, the story is told of Bar Hadaya, an interpreter of dreams who would give a favorable interpretation to one who paid him a fee and an unfavorable interpretation to one who did not. Two dreamers, Abbaye and Rava, each had the same dream on an ongoing basis. Both went to a Bar Hadaya for an interpretation of the dream, but while Abbaye paid the interpreter for his services, the second dreamer refused to do so. To the paying client, the interpreter gave a favorable interpretation; conversely, the nonpaying client was given adverse interpretations. The interpretations given to both dreamers eventually actualized. The nonpaying dreamer gradually changed his strategy and began to pay the interpreter, at which point both the interpretations and the realization of the dreams become favorable. At one time Bar Hadaya and Rava embarked on a journey together. When Bar Hadaya disembarked, he accidentally dropped a book, which Rava found. He saw written in "All dreams follow the [interpreter's] mouth." At that, Rava exclaimed, "Wretch! It all depended on you, and you caused me such great distress!

Psychoanalysis, which is to a large degree based on Freud's theories, holds that dreams are the workings of the unconscious mind, revealing a censored representation of unconscious wishes and feelings. Dream interpretation thus provides a window into the unconscious and may help to elucidate conscious psychological activity. This notion forms the foundation of much of psychoanalytic therapy.

Other theorists (Hobson and McCarley) have suggested that dreams have no useful value or significance and that they occur because of random electrical discharges emanating from the brainstem to the cortex. The "plot" of a dream results from a fabrication by the cortex in response to this random bombardment.

Still other investigators have suggested that REM sleep and dreaming are very important for brain development, which explains why infants and children (as well as fetuses) dream so much more than adults do. Proponents of this theory point out that during REM sleep, neurons are extremely active—so much so that the brain consumes more oxygen during this stage of sleep than during intense physical or mental activity during the waking state. This degree of activity presumably stimulates neurons to develop and grow, much as physical exercise stimulates the development of muscles. This is an attractive theory, but it fails to explain why adults continue to dream even after their brains have been fully developed.

Other investigators (Francis Crick and Graeme Mitchison) hold that dreams are a way of "cleansing" the brain from an overload of information accumulated during daily activity. These investigators theorize that the cortex may become overloaded by incoming information, which could result in the neocortex developing false or "parasitic" thoughts that would endanger the orderly storage of information in the brain. REM sleep serves to erase this information from the cortex on a regular basis. "We dream to forget," wrote proponents of this theory. Later they proposed that this overload of information could result in abnormal fantasies or obsessions, which are erased by dreaming.

Another interesting but disputed theory was posed by Jewett in the 1960s. As discussed, the body is paralyzed during the REM stage. Jewett placed certain lesions in a number of cats' brains, eliminating such paralysis and thus allowing the animals to "act out their dreams." During the dreaming stage of sleep, these brain-lesioned cats displayed behaviors suggestive of fighting, grooming, exploring the environment, running away, and showing rage. Jewett concluded that dreams are a way of "practicing" certain vital survival activities that are likely to be encountered in real life. Rehearsing them during dreams allows cats to perform them flawlessly when awake. Dreams thus represent a stage in which we are allowed an opportunity to rehearse wakeful existence.

Somewhat supportive of this theory are recently developed techniques that utilize imagery and visualization to help athletes perform better in sports. These athletes imagine and visualize themselves performing certain specific activities that they perform when carrying out the sport, with resultant improvement in real performance. Although it is significant that these athletes are awake while involved in the visualization, it can be argued conceptually that visualization also takes place during dreaming.

Still another theory for the purposes of dreams is that proposed by Jonathan Winston, who suggests that dreaming may be necessary for the orderly processing and storage of information that is acquired during wakefulness. The content of dreams thus expresses the type of information that is dealt with and being laid down in the brain and that frequently reflects an individual's worries, concerns, and strategies utilized to deal with the environment during wakefulness. Thus, Winston suggests that "the subjects of dreams are broad ranging and complex, incorporating self-images, fears, insecurities, strengths, grandiose ideas, sexual orientation, desire, jealousy, and love." This hypothesis also explains the differences among infants, children, and adults in terms of time spent dreaming. Infants and children dream more because their unexplored brains have so much more information to process and consolidate.

This theory also explains the onset of REM sleep at a certain stage of evolution. As discussed, the spiny anteater is the only mammal known not to experience REM sleep. However, the relative size of the prefrontal cortex in comparison to the rest of the brain is larger in this animal than in any other mammal, even humans. The prefrontal cortex plays an important role in the processing and storage of memory. Winston proposes that as animals evolved, the prefrontal cortex could have also evolved to such a degree as to become too large for the head. The onset of REM sleep at a certain stage of evolution thus provided a mechanism for more efficient memory storage and a lesser need for growth of the prefrontal cortex for that purpose.

Scientists have attempted to elucidate the purpose of dreaming by observing what happens to animals and humans if they are prevented from dreaming. In an unusual experiment exploring this issue, sleepy cats were placed on a floating surface in a container full of water. The surface was large enough for cats to curl up and sleep, but upon entering REM sleep, muscle relaxation would ensue and cause the cats to fall in the water and thus wake up. They would then crawl up on the surface and go back to sleep. After a few nights of this situation, these cats, which were deprived of dreaming but not of other stages of sleep, became more aggressive and uptight.

I can just see my distinguished readers put up their collective index finger and rightfully shout, "Wait! who *wouldn't* get aggressive and angry after a few nights of being awakened several times by falling in the water?" Perhaps that's a good point, but other studies that utilized more amiable techniques, such as gently waking the cat when REM sleep was detected on brain-wave recordings, obtained similar results.

The consequences of suppressing REM sleep in humans are less clear. Many drugs, including alcohol, diazepam (Valium), antidepressants, and other tranquilizers, suppress REM sleep, which means that people who take these agents dream less, but people who take them even for long periods of time do not appear to be seriously affected from a psychological perspective. Humans deprived of dreaming for up to 16 days by being awakened during REM sleep do not appear to suffer any signs of serious psychological disturbance, but if they are subsequently allowed to sleep uninterruptedly, they have a "rebound" increase in the amount they dream per night. The longer they are kept from dreaming, the longer they dream once they are allowed to sleep undisturbed. This suggests that dreaming fulfills some important need.

Recent studies have shown that individuals taught certain information during the day and prevented from going into REM sleep at night by being awakened only during that stage have difficulty recalling the information the following day. These studies are highly supportive of the theory that REM sleep and dreaming have an important role in memory consolidation and learning.

The Content of Dreams

A greater mystery than why we dream is what we dream. If REM sleep is associated with dreaming and babies dream even before being born, what is the content of their dreams? The truth is that the exact content of dreams is hidden to all except the dreaming individual exclusively during the time he or she is dreaming. Since no one has ever been able to visualize their own or others' dreams while awake, our only information about the content of dreams is what people remember after waking up. Recalling a dream is thus a conscious mind's interpretation and attempt to make sense of an unconscious event. The accuracy of this recall is unknown. Recall of a dream can be likened to a person being told to interpret and make up a story about an abstract painting, utilizing concrete thought patterns to relate an abstract concept. Most dreams people recall have a plot; that is, they tell a story with sequential events. Whether this is an accurate expression of the dream's content or whether it is the doings of a conscious person making sense of a series of confused images is unknown. Some writers have likened the recall of a dream to a person making up a story of what he or she sees in a Rorschach ink blot. Interestingly, studies have shown that a person's recall of the plot of a dream shortly after waking up substantially differs in substance from his account of the same dream a few hours afterward.

There is some evidence, albeit indirect, that dreams may in fact contain a plot. Long periods of REM sleep are associated with longer and more complex plots recollected when the person wakes up. This correlation between length of REM and length of recalled plots suggests that dreams indeed contain plots. Further evidence is provided by individuals who suffer from a rare condition called REM sleep disorder, discussed in detail later in the chapter. Individuals with this condition act out their dreams while asleep. When doing so, they usually carry out activities suggestive of a plot.

Studies that have looked at the content of dreams have found that most dreams are in fact unpleasant. The popular idealistic saying, "follow one's dreams," would thus not be in anyone's best interest. Calvin Hall catalogued 10,000 dreams from normal individuals and found that 64 percent were associated with sadness, apprehension, or anger. People were twice as likely to have dreams in which they were subject to murder, denunciation, or attack as they were to be subjects of friendly acts. Only 18 percent of dreams were happy or exciting, and only 1 percent of them had sexual content, with very few of these involving sexual intercourse. Supportive of data suggesting the unpleasantness of dreams is the fact that patients suffering from REM sleep disorder usually perform activities of attack or defense when acting out their dreams.

Dreams of imminent death, such as falling from a high place or being threatened with being immediately murdered, are common, but most dreamers of these situations report waking up before falling the ground or receiving a bullet. The popular legend that real-life death would occur if one were to strike the ground or receive a bullet in a dream is difficult to substantiate with the available evidence; if that were true, the dreaming person would be unable to report it.

There is strong evidence that as suggested by Freud and others, the content of dreams does have an important psychological cause. Situations or worries that occur during waking life frequently make their way into dreams. As the Talmud states, "A man is shown in a dream matters that are already in his own thoughts." In a recent study by Rosalind Cartwright, a large number of individuals who were undergoing marital separation or divorce were awakened during REM sleep and asked to report and interpret their dreams. Most subjects reported issues related to their current crises and their way of coping with them.

Are we able to voluntarily control the content of our dreams in any way? In a dramatic story by the Argentine writer Juan Luis Borgues, a man secludes himself in an abandoned temple in the middle of the jungle to perform a "difficult yet not impossible task": to dream to life the perfect man. After a number of unsuccessful attempts, some due to his inability to fall asleep, the man is able to control the course of his dreams and complete his task. In a dramatic ending, a fire traps the dreamer inside the temple. Realizing the impossibility of escape, the dreamer prepares to die, but the fire does not affect him. He then realizes with horror that he is himself the dream of another dreamer.

Signs of Malfunction

Insomnia is the chronic inability to obtain the quantity or quality of sleep necessary to adequately perform daytime activities. The causes of insomnia are many, varying from psychological factors to respiratory problems. A large proportion of patients with complaints of insomnia actually underestimate the number of hours they sleep. However, many chronic insomniacs have some abnormalities in their sleep patterns, with shorter sleep time and more frequent awakenings. An interesting characteristic of insomniacs is that they maintain higher body temperature during sleep than do normal sleepers. The cause of this phenomenon is unknown.

A rare but fascinating condition affecting certain individuals is *REM behavior disorder*. Individuals with this condition fail to become paralyzed during REM sleep, and much like the cats with brain lesions described earlier, they will literally jump out of bed and act out their dreams while asleep. This is a very dangerous condition, since affected persons acting out violent dreams frequently seriously harm themselves and their bed partners. One of my patients with this condition began violently striking a dresser while dreaming that he was being attacked by a bull on his farm. Fortunately, these patients can improve if treated with certain medications.

In *narcolepsy*, an affected individual suffers irresistible sleep attacks that last 5 to 30 minutes and frequently occur without warning and at numerous times during a day. Other patients do have warning in the form of overwhelming drowsiness preceding an attack. A second characteristic of patients with this condition are attacks of *cataplexy*, which consist of sudden paralysis, usually triggered by emotion such as anger or fear, and which often result in the patient falling to the floor. The patient suddenly and without warning finds himself fully alert and conscious but totally unable to move, a terrifying situation (akin to being buried alive) as described by some patients. One of my patients with narcolepsy would fall to the ground and be unable to move when he got into arguments with his colleagues at work. A third characteristic of narcolepsy is sleep paralysis, which consists of total paralysis affecting the conscious person lying in bed and drifting into or out of sleep. Narcolepsy is also a dangerous and frequently deadly condition since patients may fall asleep at inappropriate times, such as when driving or operating heavy machinery. This disorder is caused by the sudden intrusion of REM sleep in an awake individual. In fact, patients with narcolepsy who drift into sleep at normal bedtime hours will go immediately from being awake to being in REM sleep, which takes several minutes to hours for a normal individual. Although treatment is available, these patients must adapt their lifestyles to the disease, keeping in mind the threat of falling asleep or becoming suddenly paralyzed at unpredictable times.

Night terrors are episodes that occur usually in children. Shortly after falling asleep, a child suddenly wakes up screaming, with a terrified expression on his or her face. The episodes last 1 to 2 minutes and the child usually has no recollection of the cause for the fear, nor is any there any remembrance of the episode the next morning. There are a number of differences between night terrors and bad dreams. The latter occur in people of all ages, take place during REM sleep, contain complex imagery, and usually have a plot that is vividly remembered when a person wakes up. Night terrors occur in children, take place during slow-wave sleep, have no plot, and are poorly remembered after waking up.

Coma is a state of loss of consciousness in which a person has limited responsiveness to the environment. Coma can result from a wide number of conditions affecting neurons, some reversible and other irreversible. A comatose person appears to be asleep, but sleep and coma are very different conditions. As we have learned, the brain is very active during sleep, performing a number of activities, including dreaming, and consuming more energy than during wakefulness. In contrast, the brain in a comatose person is much less active than normal, consuming much less energy. Dreaming occurs in a very limited fashion, if at all, in a person in coma.

8 Nutrition and the Brain

What to Feed Your Brain: Food for Thought

As I was looking at a patient's chart a few days ago, a person sat down next to me and secretly showed me what looked like green fossilized reptilian eggs. "They are food for the brain," she whispered in my ear, as though revealing a profound secret. "I have been taking them for a month now. I got them through a mail-order catalogue and they are guaranteed to make you smarter and give you energy." I had to shy away from the malicious thought that she had at least shown good insight into her needs by purchasing that product, but that since the eggs had apparently had little effect, she should take advantage of the guarantee. I looked at the list of ingredients or the bottle: The eggs contained a number of herbs I had never heard of as well as different types of seaweed. The green eggs and myself eyed each other suspiciously, with evident mutual mistrust. At the person's urging, I reached out to taste one of the them, but a scream inside my head stopped me. "We" cried out my angry and offended (and I admit, somewhat neurotic and spoiled) neurons in unison, "don't do seaweed!"

A second relevant incident happened a few days later, when I was sitting in a bar drinking beer and munching potato chips. A person sitting at the other end of the bar came over to me, lifted his index finger accusingly, and gravely stated, "You are what you eat." He then proceeded to walk away. I was so impressed by his comment that I couldn't swallow the potato chips in my mouth. I had this vision of a gang of my neurons sitting in a bar drinking beer and stuffing their nuclei with greasy, salty potato chips.

It's interesting to note that so much emphasis is given to the concept that you somehow become what you eat. For example, one of the reasons given by the philosopher Maimonides for the dietary laws of Judaism was that you must avoid eating animals whose characteristics you do not want to emulate. Thus, eating birds of prey must be avoided so as not to emulate the birds' aggressive qualities. Certain cultures of New Zealand eat the brain of the dead to incorporate some of the deceased person's qualities. Certain tribes in Africa also eat the liver of their enemies to incorporate their courage, and to many Europeans, eating the liver of deer also increases courage.

In the case of the brain, you really are not what you eat, due to the fact that the brain is extremely selective as to what it allows its neurons to come in contact with. Therefore, in dealing with the subject of nutrition and the brain, two important topics emerge. The first is how much of what you ingest actually gets to the brain; the second is what the brain needs for nutrition.

Several factors determine what nutrients get you the brain. The first is what you eat. The second factor is how much of a substance that you have ingested survives the attack by the acid in your stomach. The third factor is how much of the remaining substance is absorbed by the alimentary tract (the stomach and intestines) and is delivered to the bloodstream. The bloodstream is the body's road system, carrying material around the body. The fourth factor is how much of a substance that has made its way to the bloodstream gets taken up by the liver and *metabolized* (which basically means broken down and destroyed) before it even makes it to the brain. The fifth factor is how much of a substance that actually reaches the brain is taken up from the bloodstream and delivered to neurons.

Let's suppose that you hear that substance A (subA) is good for the brain. You diligently go to the health food store and buy subA capsules, which you take that night. Your stomach cells decide that subA may be good for you and absorb 20 percent of it, letting the other 80 percent be excreted. The stomach cells then deliver what's left of subA to the bloodstream, where it happily swims along until it gets to the liver. The liver cells decide they don't really like subA that much and they manage to capture 80 percent of it from the bloodstream and destroy it. The frightened molecules that survive this liver aggression continue frantically swimming in the bloodstream until they reach the brain. There, before subA gets even close to a neuron, it must pass the formidable barrier between the bloodstream and the neurons called the *blood brain barrier*, or BBB.

THE BLOOD/BRAIN BARRIER

The BBB can be conceptualized as a massive wall, similar to those that surrounded ancient cities (Figure 8-1). Inside the walls are the brain cells; outside is the bloodstream. For any substance to approach the brain cells, it must surpass those walls. Along the walls are multiple doors leading to the inside, but all doors are watched by zealous guards. In the vicinity of the

FIGURE 8-1   The blood brain barrier provides formidable, heavily "guarded" barrier between the bloodstream and the brain.

doors tiny men (called *carriers*) hang around, watching the bloodstream closely. Every few moments these carriers see something they want in the bloodstream and they swim toward it, grabbing it and carrying it inside the walls. Thus, for a molecule swimming in the bloodstream to gain access to the brain cells, it must surpass the walls in one of three ways: It must be allowed in by the guards (called *passive transport*, since there's no work performed by the carriers); it must be carried inside by the carriers (called *active transport*, since activity or work is performed by the carriers), or it must force itself in by tricking the guards or breaking the walls (Figure 8-2).

Ironically, commonly abused drugs, including heroine, nicotine, alcohol, and diazepam (Valium), are allowed to enter the brain by passive

FIGURE 8-2 Schematic representation of the blood/brain barrier. On the left side we can visualize the process of passive transport. Oxygen molecules, as well as heroin and alcohol, are allowed to enter undisturbed (A). On the right side we see the process of active transport. Glucose molecules are carried in by carriers (B). Bacteria (PC) and other organisms frequently enter the brain by breaking down the blood/brain barrier (C).

transport; that is, they are allowed by the guards to enter the walls rapidly and without restriction. For example, when a person smokes a cigarette, nicotine that enters the bloodstream from the lungs appears in the brain within 3 to 4 seconds. Likewise, heroin injected into the bloodstream also appears in the brain within seconds to minutes. This rapid entrance of these substances into the brain accounts for their very rapid onset of effect and may account for their potential for abuse.

Glucose, on the other hand, is not allowed by the guards to enter the walls; instead, it is carried in at very large concentrations by the carriers. This frenzy that carriers have to bring glucose into the brain is due its importance as the brain's main energy source. Entry to the brain by means of carriers also occurs with many other essential nutrients utilized by the brain.

Organisms, including bacteria and viruses, enter the brain from the bloodstream by literally breaking down the walls, but the mechanism by which they do so is unknown. Brain tumors also break down the BBB, presumably to permit rapid extraction of nutrients from the blood, thus enhancing the growth of a tumor.

All of these steps that a substance must go through before reaching the brain mean that only a fraction of what a person ingests ever makes it to the neurons. This holds true for all elements, including nutrients, drugs, or vitamins. In fact, this is one of the challenges facing drug designers in the pharmaceutical business. If one wants a drug to reach the brain, it must be designed so that it passes successfully through all five steps of the BBB.

Indeed, bypassing one of the steps that normally keep a drug from reaching the neuron can result in successful delivery of the drug to the brain. For example, heroin is destroyed by the stomach if taken by mouth, but if injected into the bloodstream, it easily reaches neurons, a fact well known to drug abusers. Similarly, morphine does not penetrate the BBB well, but heroin, a derivative of morphine, penetrates it easily.

In fact, a small change in the chemical structures of many drugs can enable them to reach brain cells. That is the case with levodopa, a drug used in the treatment of Parkinson's disease. Dopamine is a neurotransmitter that has been shown to be decreased in the brains of persons suffering from Parkinson's disease. If dopamine is ingested, it is absorbed from the stomach into the bloodstream, but it does not penetrate the BBB. It is thus of no use in the treatment of this condition. However, levodopa is utilized by brain cells to manufacture dopamine. Levodopa easily penetrates the BBB and has become one of the mainstays in the treatment of patients suffering from Parkinson's.

Unfortunately, we know of many genetic diseases of the brain that are caused by a deficit of a particular element that can be easily manufactured in a laboratory, but in most of those diseases, no one has figured out how to deliver those elements to brain cells or to force neurons to take up those substances once they are in the bloodstream.

This selectivity of the brain for choosing nutrients is also important to consider when we contemplate spending thousands of dollars on vitamins or other elements that manufacturers want us to believe are helpful for brain function. Even if it is true that those elements are necessary, chances are that ingesting them by mouth will not result in them ever reaching neurons.

NUTRIENTS NEEDED BY THE BRAIN

Before we expand on the topic of the brain and nutrition, it is important to stress a few points. Our current knowledge of the type of nutrients the brain needs to develop, grow, and function is overshadowed by the lack of knowledge about the subject. At best, we have an incomplete understanding of what elements are good or bad for the brain, and even this limited understanding fluctuates throughout the years. We are only too familiar with reports from both medical and nonmedical sources advocating certain nutrients one year and reversing that recommendation a few years later.

Additionally, we must be careful in interpreting media reports that advocate or disparage nutrients for the brain, since many of these reports have little scientific basis. Much of our factual knowledge about the brain and nutrition stems from scientists observations of animals and humans that have been deprived of a certain substance, as we will discuss. Claims in the nonmedical media that are not backed up by rigorous research should be interpreted with the utmost care.

Finally, although we have identified certain nutrients the brain needs for development and function, this does not mean that an excess of that particular nutrient will be beneficial to the brain. In fact, the converse can also be true: too much of a necessary nutrient, such as in the case of vitamin C or A, can actually be detrimental to the brain. For the most part, however, the brain will use only the amount of a nutrient that it needs and will discard the excess. Thus, if you take in too much of a nutrient, you will be wasting money, since the excess will not be stored or used by the brain and will end up being discarded in the urine (which has led to the term "expensive urine," referring to the urine full of costly vitamins and nutrients in individuals who ingest excessive amount of these).

In order to better understand the types of nutrient needed by the brain, we can use the following analogy. In previous sections we pointed out that the main function of neurons is to communicate with other neurons and that this communication takes place through means of neurotransmitters. Most of these neurotransmitters are manufactured within the neurons themselves. Therefore, for purposes of our discussion of nutrition and the brain, we can compare a neuron to an infinitely sophisticated manufacturing plant, where the main manufactured products are neurotransmitters.

For the building, repair, and daily operation of any manufacturing plant, three categories of material are needed. The first are substances needed to build and maintain the plant itself. The second are raw materials from which to produce the finished product. The third is fuel necessary for everyday functioning. These categories are discussed in the following sections.

Fuel

The brain is a ravenous consumer of energy. In comparison to the other organs of the body, it is a voracious eater. Although the brain accounts for less than 2 percent of a person's weight, it consumes 20 percent of the body's energy. At the same time, the brain is an extremely picky eater. For example, most cells in the body can use a variety of elements as fuel (or energy sources), including a number of carbohydrates, such as glucose and fructose. Additionally, most cells of the body can store and even convert fats into fuel if they need to. In contrast, neurons can utilize only glucose; except for some exceptional circumstances such as prolonged starvation, they are unable to use anything else. Furthermore, nerve cells cannot store glucose in their bodies; they must get it from the bloodstream at the precise moment they are going to use it. If they are unable to immediately get glucose, nerve cells will stop functioning, such as occurs when one loses consciousness or passes out after a prolonged fast. Total absence of glucose (an extremely rare situation), even for a short amount of time, results in the death of the neurons, since they are unable to store fat and convert it to fuel when needed, as other cells are able to do. Thus, glucose is to the brain as a parachute is to a skydiver—if it's not there when needed, chances are it will never be needed again.

Building Material

It would be little presumptuous to even attempt to enumerate the vast amount of materials required for normal development, upkeep, and repair of neurons, partly because we have limited knowledge of the subject and partly because it would require entire volumes containing little factual information and much speculation. Here limit ourselves to enumerating certain concepts that are central to a discussion of nutrition and list some nutrients that have been identified by scientific studies to be important for the brain.

Much like with the building of a plant, where certain materials are needed at certain precise stages of the building process, the body requires certain specific materials at discrete stages during the development of the brain. The lack of high-quality materials at the time they are needed could lead to a deficient end product. These precise stages, called *critical periods*, exist throughout the lifetime of an individual. Thus, the human embryo, the child and young adult, and the aging individual require different specific nutrients for the development and repair of neurons. However, much like the building of a plant, the neuron requires much of its necessary building material early in the building or development process.

Iodine, for example, is an important nutrient that is particularly important for normal brain development in children. A number of vitamins are necessary for brain development and maintenance. Such is the case for vitamins B1 and B12 and folic acid. The lack of any of these vitamins at various stages of a person's life can result in serious neurological disorders. For example, lack of folic acid and vitamin B12 can lead to serious damage to neurons that is expressed clinically as depression, dementia, and problems with movement and walking.

Another group of nutrients that have received much attention in scientific circles in recent years is the antioxidants, which are substances that have the potential to reduce the damaging effects of many processes. During normal function, the neurons and glial cells produce certain waste products that can be toxic to cells. Antioxidants have the capacity to neutralize those noxious substances. The value of these agents is still being debated.

NEUROTRANSMITTERS

Neurotransmitters are manufactured within neurons in an assembly-line fashion (Figure 8-3). Most of the work is performed by chemical workers called *enzymes*, which take the raw products and either add or take away substances from them and pass them on to the next enzyme until the finished neurotransmitter is assembled. At the end of the assembly line, the finished product is conveniently stored in packages called *vesicles*, which are easy to ship throughout the cell.

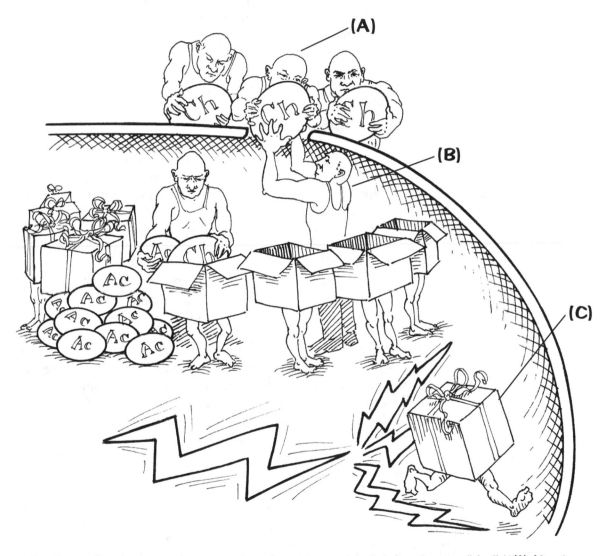

FIGURE 8-3   Manufacture of neurotransmitters. Raw products are brought in from the extracellular fluid (A). After the neurotransmitter is manufactured, it is packaged into vesicles (B) and later released into the synaptic space (C) as detailed in the section on neurotransmission in prior chapters.

The number of neurotransmitters manufactured depends on a number of factors. First, there must be an adequate amount of raw product inside the neuron. Figure 8-3 shows examples of raw products necessary to manufacture specific neurotransmitters.

Second, the number of neurotransmitters manufactured depends on the number of chemical workers available to work in the manufacturing process. Because the neuron has relatively little control over the amount of available raw product, this second step is the main mechanism by which it regulates the amount of neurotransmitter fabricated. This phase is frequently referred to as the *rate-limiting step*, because under normal circumstances, there is an ample supply of raw product. The number of enzymes available to perform the work determines how many neurotransmitters are brought to completion. Think of a manufacturing plant that builds plastic toys. In a situation in which there is ample supply of plastic, the number of workers available to change the raw plastic into toys will determine how many toys are built.

This being said, there is ample evidence that diet does modify to a certain degree, the number of neurotransmitters in the brain. This is a fascinating area of research, one of which we will hear more in the next few years, but some of the data available to date is summarized here.

The role of diet upon the neurotransmitter acetylcholine has been widely studied because much is known about its synthesis and because it has been implicated in a number of functions of the brain, especially memory. Additionally, the deficit of acetylcholine has been implicated in disorders of the brain, especially Alzheimer's disease. The idea that diet could affect the amount of acetylcholine in the brain has thus generated much attention.

Choline and lecithin are the main raw products necessary for the production of acetylcholine. Both are widely present in a number of food products, especially liver, peanuts, iceberg lettuce, and cauliflower. Choline is also present in high concentrations in maternal milk, suggesting that it is a fundamental product necessary for brain development. However, not all of the choline that neurons utilize to manufacture acetylcholine comes from the diet. A small amount is manufactured by neurons themselves, and some is recycled from the breakdown of membranes. However, a large percentage stems from ingested choline. In fact, research has shown that the ingestion of both lecithin and choline leads to a rapid increase in the amount of acetylcholine in the brain.

Studies that have looked at the role of dietary choline on functions of the brain have taken one of two approaches. The first is to investigate the effects of decreased dietary choline on memory. These studies, performed in rats, showed that deficits of choline in the diet lead to disorders of memory. Other studies that have looked at the effect of increased dietary choline have shown that the supplanting of choline in the normal diet of the rat leads to the rat's improved performance in tasks that require memory. Furthermore, choline supplements seem especially useful if they are given during certain times in a rat's life. These times consist of the embryonic days 12–17 and the postnatal days 16–30, which correspond to the times when neurons or connections between neurons are being formed. This is an excellent illustration of the concept of critical periods; certain nutrients are necessary during a specific stage of development. The deficit of these nutrients during those periods of time could have irreversible consequences.

The role of dietary deficits or supplanting of choline on functions of the brain in humans is much less clear. However, to date there is no clear evidence suggesting that the dietary supplanting of choline leads to improvement in memory disorders such as Alzheimer's Disease, or to a decrease in the normally occurring memory loss that accompanies age. However, there is some evidence that choline or lecithin may improve memory among otherwise normal young people with relatively poor memory functions. Much more research is needed, but I predict that future research will show benefits of dietary choline on functions of the brain, especially memory.

The role of diet in modifying the concentration of neurotransmitters in the brain has been studied for other neurotransmitters such as serotonin, a neurotransmitter that has been implicated in certain psychiatric diseases, including depression and mania, and in the regulation of sleep, pain, and aggression. Serotonin appears to especially important in the induction and maintenance of sleep. The precursor for serotonin is the essential amino acid tryptophan, which it is found in most protein-containing foods, especially warm milk. Although the relationship between the supplementing of tryptophan and the concentration of serotonin in the brain is not totally clear, many studies have documented that ingesting tryptophan increases sleep and aids patients who have insomnia. Some scientific evidence also suggests that tryptophan may be helpful in treating some patients who suffer from depression. All of these findings suggest that the oral intake of tryptophan may increase the concentration of serotonin in the brain.

Another neurotransmitter that may potentially be affected by diet is norepinephrine. Among its multiple functions, this neurotransmitter appears to have an important role in the regulation of mood, especially in the control of anxiety and stress. Some animal studies reveal that under stress, the concentration of norepinephrine in the brain decreases, suggesting that the brain utilizes more of it when it is faced with stressful situations. When the concentration of norepinephrine in the brain of rats decreases, behaviors that include exploring, learning, eating, drinking, and sleeping are also affected.

Tyrosine, a substance found in many food products, is the precursor of norepinephrine. The relationship between the ingestion of tyrosine and the concentration of norepinephrine in the brain is not certain. However, single doses of tyrosine given to acutely stressed animals counteract the stressing effects of electrical shocks. Furthermore, animals pretreated with tyrosine do not exhibit shock-induced impairments in exploratory behavior. In addition, the norepinephrine levels in the brains of these animals do not appear to decrease with increased stress. A short-term tyrosine diet has also been shown to improve motor activity in old mice, which has been attributed to an increase of dopamine activity. All of this data suggests that tyrosine, taken orally, may increase the level of norepinephrine in the brain. As is often the case, the evidence for the beneficial role of tyrosine to humans is less clear. When administered to young, unstressed people, tyrosine appears to have little effect on behavior, but there is evidence that it has beneficial effects on mood in older individuals.

9 Drug Abuse and the Brain

A few years ago a commercial on television caught my attention. If my memory storage within my temporal lobes serve me correctly, I recall that it began by showing two whole eggs while an announcer sternly decreed in a grave voice. "This is your brain." This was followed by the image of two eggs being fried in a sizzling frying pan while the announcer again announced, "This is your brain on drugs." Shortly afterward, I saw a poster that showed an image of two eggs being fried in a sizzling pan along with two strips of bacon. The caption below the image announced, "This is your brain on drugs and with a side of bacon."

The commercial was, if nothing else, interesting. As a neuroscientist I take some issue with the brain being compared to a pair of eggs (I imagine that each egg is supposed to represent a hemisphere), but there is no denying that the conveyed message, although lacking in style, probably made many people think. It could indeed be argued that a sizzling frying pan is to eggs what drugs are to your brain.

Drugs don't really fry your brain, but they certainly can affect its function, at times on a permanent basis. But what are "recreational" drugs? They are potent pharmacological agents that contain the ability to temporarily or permanently affect our perception of reality. In this property lies their appeal and their danger.

Much of our brain's energy is devoted to guiding and regulating our conscious perception of that complex external universe we call reality. As we have discussed, perception is the mechanism by which the brain obtains and processes information about elements external to itself and comes up with a mental representation of these elements. The brain concerns itself with both the quantity and the quality of perception, that is, how much and what we perceive. To correctly perceive the external universe, the brain recruits many organs and allies, including all the senses, past experiences, and memory and knowledge stores. The perceived image is not a mirror image of reality; everything we perceive contains a portion of ourselves.

To explain this better, let's review some concepts that we discussed in prior sections. Let's suppose Anatole is walking down the street and suddenly sees a lion. The mental image that Anatole makes of that lion contains various components. First is the registration of the physical characteristics of the lion, its size, the color of its hair, its smell, and its roar. Utilizing this information, Anatole's memory stores instantly identify the object in front of him as a lion; he remembers what he knows about lions and immediately recalls that they are dangerous animals. Another component is the affective aspect, which includes what he feels about lions in general and about this lion in particular. The image of the lion may awaken fear, surprise, excitement, and awe at its beauty. Utilizing all of this data, Anatole's brain transduces an external reality, a lion, into an internal reality, his very own mental image of that lion. The internal representation that Anatole makes of the lion is comprehensive, including many components. He cannot willingly separate the components of the mental image. He cannot choose to see the image and not identify it as a lion, nor can be elect to just see it and not hear it. He is unable to see the lion and choose not to experience his feelings about it. In sum, the mental image of an external reality incorporates an infinite number of components, all intermingled, to come up with an internal reality unique to each individual. Anatole's mental lion is unlike any other lion in the universe. This mental perception Anatole has made of the lion will help him decide as to what to do next. Consequently, it is extremely important that Anatole's perception is correct, because it will guide his subsequent behavior. He may decide to run or to approach the lion. If his perception is inaccurate, his reaction may also be erroneous.

Such is the human condition. Appropriate behavior in response to reality is dependent upon a correct perception of that reality. Drugs have the potential to affect the highly complex mechanism by which we perceive the external or internal universe. They have the capacity to dull, exaggerate, or distort an individual's perception. A person may perceive more or less than is there. Colors or smells may become stronger or weaker or may contain unusual characteristics. A person may even perceive what's not even there. In summary, drugs interfere with the correct mental representation of what a person sees, feels, or remembers. This erroneous perception of an external reality also leads to an erroneous action upon that reality. This explains the aberrant behavior displayed by many drug abusers.

"Reality is overrated," claimed a slightly tipsy friend of mine while savoring some excellent South American wine. For a variety of reasons, drug users strive to distort, if only temporarily, their perception of reality. But the appeal of at least some recreational drugs may be much more fundamental than their ability to distort an individual's perception of the external universe. Recent research suggests that in fact, drugs may be involved in one of the most significant driving forces in humans: the attainment of reward or pleasure.

Recent evidence suggests that within the brain are certain areas and circuits that are involved in the feelings of reward and pleasure. These centers have been well identified in animals and, to a lesser degree, in humans. If electrodes are placed in those areas and an animal is taught to electrically stimulate itself by pressing a lever, it will cross an electric grid until it reaches exhaustion in order to do so. Animals will not cross the same grid to obtain food or water, even when starving.

The neurotransmitter dopamine appears to have an important role in communication between neurons in those pleasure areas. As we will learn later, cocaine and perhaps other drugs are able to modify the amounts of dopamine in certain areas of the brain, which could implicate them in this brain-pleasure system and may explain their abuse potential. Indeed, recent research highly supports the notion that a number of commonly abused drugs may play a role in the brain's pleasure or reward centers.

The effects of drugs on human perception, motivation, or pleasure result from the interaction between drugs and neurons. In this chapter, we discuss some characteristics of this interaction.

DRUGS AND NEURONS

Before exerting their action upon neurons, recreational drugs must reach the bloodstream, which is the roadway to the brain. Drugs reach the blood from either the intestinal system (when ingested), from the lungs (when inhaled or smoked), or by being directly injected into the veins. Once in the bloodstream, the drugs are immediately taken into the brain by the process of passive transfer, which we discussed in the section on the blood/brain barrier. A common characteristic of most recreational drugs is the short period of latency between their use and the onset of their action upon the brain. Thus, nicotine reaches the brain within seconds of being smoked. Heroin is also found in the brain within seconds or minutes of being injected into the veins. This short interval between intake and action is one of the reasons for the attractiveness of recreational drugs: immediate pleasure.

The power contained in drugs to affect the functions of the brain lies in their ability to affect the communication among neurons, which is, as we have pointed out many times, the essence of brain function. Drugs affect neuronal communication by altering the level of neurotransmitters in the brain, by modifying the way that neurons respond to these variances in neurotransmitter levels, or by themselves acting upon various neurotransmitter receptors. Different drugs affect different neurotransmitter systems. It is beyond the scope of this manual to discuss how all commonly used drugs affect the brain, but because I believe that exploring the drug/neuronal interaction teaches us much about brain function, we will discuss a few examples.

Before we do so, it is important to consider that a characteristic common to most drugs is that they affect the brain differently, whether they are taken for short periods of times or whether they are used for longer periods. Prolonged use of many drugs leads to changes in the structure and function of the brain, which lead to tolerance, sensitization, and withdrawal, concepts that are discussed in detail later in the chapter.

Benzodiazepines, which include drugs such as Valium, Librium, and alcohol, work by acting upon a neurotransmitter system called the GABA (Gamma Amyl Butyric Acid) system. We have previously discussed that some neurotransmitters are stimulatory and others are inhibitory. That is, some neurotransmitters cause the neuron to depolarize and others suppress depolarization. GABA is one of the most important inhibitory neurotransmitters. Benzodiazepines will not directly stimulate the GABA receptors, but they will cause them to become more sensitive to the effects of GABA. The net result will be higher inhibition, or decreased activity upon many cells. Activation of GABA receptors by ingestion of drugs has a number of results, including sedation, relaxation, and behavioral desinhibition.

Cocaine works by different mechanisms. We have previously discussed that an important mechanism for the elimination of a neurotransmitter from the synapse is the reuptake system. In this system, the same cell that secreted the neurotransmitter reabsorbs it and thus prevents the repeat depolarization of the postsynaptic cell. Cocaine binds to presynaptic dopaminergic receptors and thus prevents the reuptake of dopamine (Figure 9-1). The net effect is to increase the concentration of dopa-

FIGURE 9-1   Cocaine prevents the reuptake of dopamine into the presynaptic neuron. This results in an increase in the level of dopamine in the synapse. Additionally, cocaine blocks the feedback system so that the presynaptic neuron continues manufacturing and releasing dopamine into the synapse, eventually leading to exhaustion of the cell.

mine present in the synapse, prolonging its activity in stimulating the post-synaptic cell. As we discussed earlier, higher levels of dopamine in certain areas of the brain may be responsible for feelings of reward and pleasure and may also result in numerous experiential impressions, including euphoria, excitement, increased energy, and feelings of well-being, as well as other poorly defined sensations.

Opiates (which include drugs such as morphine and heroin) affect communication between neurons in a fascinating manner. As with all other functions of the brain, there are neurons in the brain which are responsible for the transmission and conscious feeling of pain. For ease of discussion, we refer to these neurons as *pain-processing neurons*, or PPN. These PPN contain receptors (called *opioid receptors*) to which opiates attach themselves. Other neurotransmitters, including endorphins and enkephalins, also act upon these same receptors. The attachment of opiates to opioid receptors causes an interesting change in PPN. The neurons undergo a state called *hyperpolarization*, which means that they become less responsive or dulled to stimulation by other cells. The conscious perception of pain results from neurons transmitting impulses from the pain source to the brain and the correct interpretation by PPN of those impulses. The net result of hyperpolarization of PPN is that they will be less effective in transmitting or depolarizing in response to a painful stimuli, which will decrease an individual's conscious feeling of pain. Besides relief from pain, opiates will also produce sedation, relaxation, mental cloudiness, and other poorly classified feelings of well-being.

TOLERANCE

When neurons are exposed to the presence of drugs for longer periods, they become accustomed to them; that is, in a way they learn to adapt to their presence. Why do they do this? Probably because neurons realize that without this adaptation, the abnormal activation to which drugs subject them would seriously interfere with their vitality. This adaptation is therefore a matter of survival. Unlike you, neurons are unable to "just say no to drugs," or if they can, most drug users pretend not to hear them. Unable to prevent drugs presence, neurons are forced to learn how to live with them. They do this by a process called *neuroadaptation*.

Neurons adapt to the constant presence of drugs by finding new ways of reacting to them. One of the ways is by developing *tolerance* to the drug. Tolerance is defined as the body's compensatory diminution in the response to a given dose of a drug, so that a larger dose is required to achieve the same effect. To achieve tolerance, the neuron does not work alone; it recruits other organs of the body. For example, by means of a process called *metabolic tolerance*, the neurons recruit the liver, which becomes more adept at destroying the drug before it reaches the brain. That explains the increased resistance of habitual alcohol drinkers to the intoxicating effects of alcohol. Their liver cells have become expert at destroying a large proportion of the alcohol before it reaches the brain. Other areas of the body learn to destroy or metabolize the drug faster so that there is less concentration of the drug to affect the brain.

Another process by which tolerance is achieved is called *cellular adaptation* (Figures 9-2, 9-3, 9-4, and 9-5). Neurons themselves learn to react less to a drug via a number of mechanisms, some of them not well understood. One way this happens is by modifying the number of receptors so that there is a lesser number to which to respond the increased volume of neurotransmitters affected by the drug. Another way is by modifying the sensitivity, that is, the response that receptors have to neurotransmitters, resulting in decreased stimulation in response to the abnormally increased number of neurotransmitters. Neurotransmitters still bind to receptors, but no response by the postsynaptic cell takes place. These two mechanisms are extremely

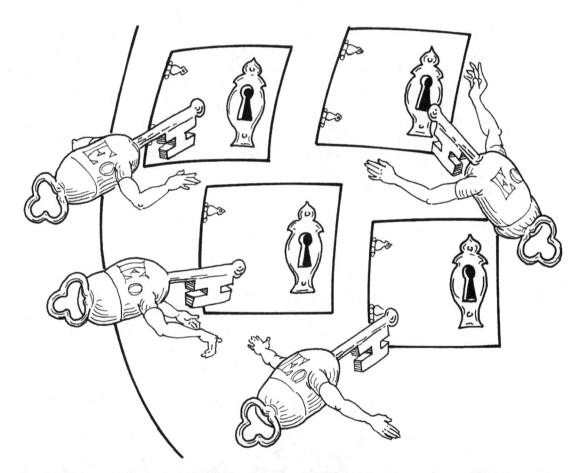

FIGURES 9-2, 9-3, 9-4, AND 9-5   Tolerance and withdrawal. Normally there is an equilibrium between the number of endogenous opioid molecules and receptors (Figure 9-2). With the ingestion of exogenous opioids, there is an oversupply of opioids in relation to the number of receptors (Figure 9-3). To compensate, the postsynaptic neuron reduces its number of receptors so as to decrease excessive activation by the excess of opioids (Figure 9-4). The production of endogenous opioids is also reduced. Therefore, a new equilibrium is reached between the number of opioid receptors and opioid molecules. When the ingestion of endogenous opioids is suddenly discontinued, there is an undersupply of endogenous opioids and of postsynaptic endogenous receptors (Figure 9-5). This leads to the clinical symptoms of withdrawal. Eventually, both the number of opioid receptors as well as the production of endogenous opioids increase, and a new equilibrium is reached.

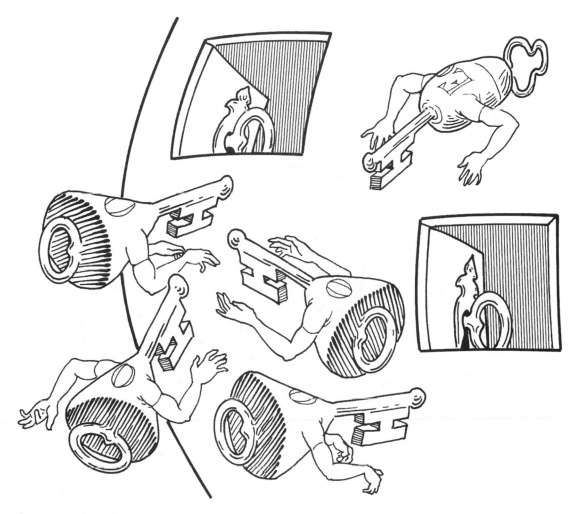

FIGURE 9-3

important in the neuronal development of tolerance and are present when alcohol, benzodiazepines, opiates, or nicotine are continually used.

Tolerance at a neuronal level is not well understood for all drugs. For example, the underlying neuronal mechanisms responsible for tolerance to cocaine, amphetamines, and other psychostimulants have not been identified. One not yet substantiated theory regarding tolerance to cocaine sustains that when cocaine binds to the presynaptic membrane and prevents the reuptake of dopamine, a major source of raw material for synthesis of new dopamine is eliminated. This is because the presynaptic neuron recycles dopamine that has been reuptaken for synthesis of new neurotransmitter. This causes a considerable reduction in the neuron's reserves of dopamine, decreasing the number of neurotransmitters the presynaptic neuron is able to secrete into the synapse. Consequently, a higher dose of cocaine is necessary to block the reuptake of dopamine, thus increasing the number of available neurotransmitters to attach to postsynaptic receptors.

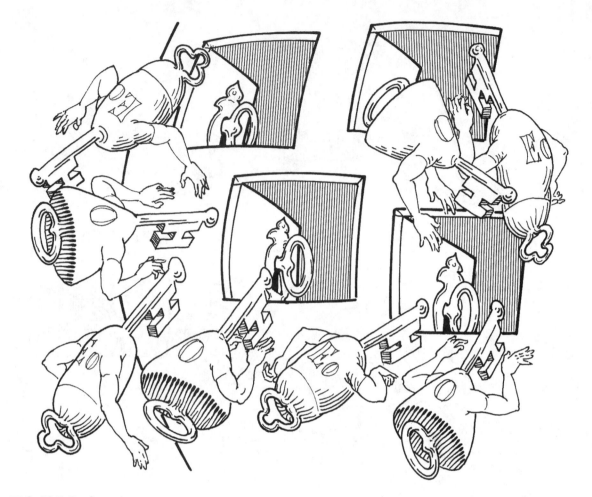

FIGURE 9-4

An important point to consider is that of crossed tolerance. Many different drugs act upon the same receptors and cause the same type of neuroadaptation. That is the case for alcohol and benzodiazepines (Valium), both of which act on the GABA neurotransmitter and receptor system. With chronic use of either drug, tolerance develops simultaneously. The same holds true for different opiates, such as morphine, heroin, and methadone. In fact, this is the basis for treating heroin addicts with methadone (with little success, I may add).

Although most individuals develop tolerance to many drugs with chronic use, the opposite can occur in some people, especially with the use of cocaine or amphetamines. By means of this process, called *sensitization*, an individual's response to the drug *increases* with subsequent use, even when the dosage remains constant. This occurs because at the cellular level, a neuron's response to the neurotransmitter secreted by the action of the drug actually increases with subsequent dosages. The mechanism responsible for sensitization is interesting. As we have discussed, presynaptic neurons contain receptors for the same neurotransmitters that they secrete when they depolarize. These presynaptic receptors, which function

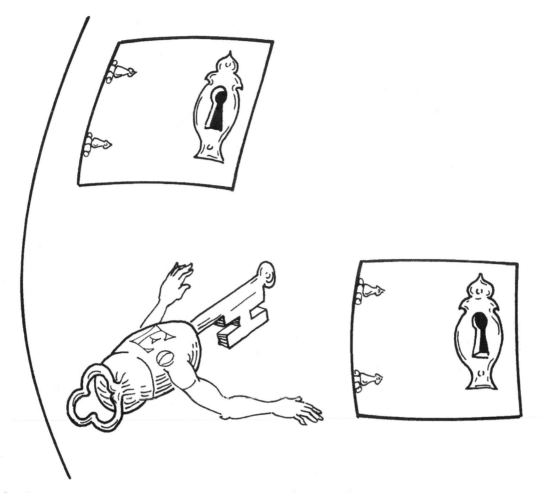

FIGURE 9-5

much like a speaker's ears, provide feedback to the presynaptic cell about the number of neurotransmitters present in the synapse. Cocaine binds to the dopamine receptors present in dopaminergic presynaptic neurons and thus prevents the binding of synaptic dopamine, desensitizing the cell and preventing it from obtaining feedback. This tricks the cell into secreting additional dopamine into the synapse, increasing the stimulation to the postsynaptic cell. The analogy can be used of a person with decreased hearing who screams when she converses because she is unable to monitor the volume of her words and speaks loudly in an attempt to hear herself.

WITHDRAWAL

With the rise of changes in the structure and function of neurons that lead to drug tolerance, neurons reach a state of normality in spite of the abnormal environment caused by the drugs. Neurons thus become dependent on the presence of drugs and unable to function normally without them.

When a drug is suddenly withdrawn, neurons are at a loss. They are suddenly faced with an environment they are no longer equipped to handle. For example, take the case of opiates. When a person takes opiates for the first time, the opiate molecules reach the brain and attach to opiate receptors present in certain brain cells. The attachment causes the neurons to hyperpolarize, or as we stated before, to become dulled to the stimulation by other cells. Once the opiate molecules leave the receptor, the cell reaches its normal state once more. But if the person continues to take opiates, those opiate receptors are continuously stimulated by the steady presence of opiates. The constantly hyperpolarized cell realizes that this is not a normal state and therefore attempts to reach a state of normality by a number of mechanisms. One mechanism is to decrease its number of opiate receptors; the second is to decrease the response of the opiate receptors to the opiate molecule. The cell then reaches a normal state in spite of the high concentration of opiates and becomes dependent on the presence of opiates. Thus, if a person wanted to obtain the same effect as with the first dose, he or she would need to take more of the drug so as to increase its concentration in the brain and override the protective mechanisms devised by the neuron. The cell has thus developed tolerance to the drug.

Now, what happens if the person suddenly stops taking opiates? Due to the prior high presence of opiates, opioid receptors in PPN become less responsive to both ingested opiates and to other "natural opiates," including endorphins and enkephalins. A balance is reached with high levels of opiates and decreased response by the opioid receptors. The sudden withdrawal of opiates disrupts this balance. Suddenly there are low levels of opiates along with decreased sensitivity of the receptors. As stated, when opiates attach themselves to opioid receptors, the result is a decrease in activity of PPN. Because there is no longer enough opiate to maintain this level, the PPN becomes too excitable, increasing its activity. This results in the person's increased perception of pain, even to minor stimulation. Because opioid receptors are also important in other functions aside from pain, other life-threatening symptoms occur with sudden withdrawal. Eventually, after several days, neurons again reach a balance, adjusting to the new situation. They do this by a mechanism that is the reverse of tolerance. The PPN increases the number and sensitivity of opioid receptors so that the cell becomes more sensitive to natural opiates. A new state of normality is reached.

Withdrawal from benzodiazepines and alcohol follows a similar course. Chronic attachment of these drugs to GABA receptors results in a compensatory decrease in the number and sensitivity of GABA receptors, until a balance similar to that of opiates is reached. Sudden withdrawal of alcohol destroys the balance. Since GABA is also an inhibitory neurotransmitter, decreased activity of receptors along with low levels of alcohol will result in increased excitability. This can result in many life-threatening withdrawal symptoms such as seizures.

The reason cocaine abusers go into withdrawal is much less clear, since the mechanisms for tolerance to cocaine at a neuronal level are not well understood. Psychological factors seem to have a greater role with cocaine than with other drugs.

LONG-TERM EFFECTS OF DRUGS ON NEURONS

The use of drugs can be associated with a number of conditions affecting basically all organs of the body. The effect of chronic drug use on neurons themselves is not well understood for all drugs.

However, there is good evidence that many drugs do harm neurons on a permanent basis. For example, long-term use of alcohol results in permanent damage to the brain, which is more pronounced in certain areas, including the cerebellum and the mammillary bodies. This damage results in specific irreversible symptoms, including problems with balance, severe memory deficits, and frank dementias. A triad of alteration in eye movements, severe cognitive changes, and ataxia, denominated Wernicke's encephalopathy, constitutes a severe condition that occurs in alcoholics. It is believed to be caused by damage to areas in the thalamus and limbic areas, resulting from severe thiamine deficiency associated with chronic alcoholism. Korsakoff's syndrome is an irreversible condition that also occurs in chronic alcoholics and causes severe memory and other cognitive deficits. Irreversible problems with memory have also been associated with long-term use of PCP and other drugs.

10 Aggression and the Brain

A nursery school teacher recently told an interesting story during a social gathering. A four-year-old child in her class struck another child in the face during an altercation over a toy. In response to the subsequent scolding by the teacher, the child asserted with an innocent smile, "My brain made me do it." By her account of the incident, the teacher sought to obtain a laugh from those listening to her story at the gathering, which understandably explains her surprise and annoyance at my remarking that the child was indeed correct. All behavior, including aggression, originates in the brain.

Not until recently have we begun to understand the interaction between brain function and aggression. Considering the degree of aggression in our society, this is an area of neuroscience that necessitates extensive research. Much remains to be discovered, but this chapter briefly summarizes our present state of knowledge.

THE DEFINITION OF AGGRESSION

The definition of aggression has a number of connotations too broad to consider in this manual. But for the purpose of our discussion, we define an act of aggression as a purposeful act committed by one individual that contains the potential to cause physical or psychological damage to that or another individual.

Ecclesiastes states, "A season is set for everything, a time for every experience under heaven." Such is the case for all of the behaviors displayed by all species, including aggression. Aggressive acts committed under certain circumstances are clearly normal, while the same act committed under another set of circumstances is aberrant. Animals performing aggressive acts to feed or to protect young or territory are displaying normal behavior, but when survival needs are not evident in the performance of aggressive acts, the normality of the behavior is in question. The differentiation between abnormal and normal aggression in humans is even more confusing. Killing another human being is "normal" in a war situation and is abnormal at any other time. I am reminded of a story told by a friend of mine who was held in a prison camp where he was tortured on a constant basis during a civil war. When peace was declared, the commander of the camp, a sadistic and cruel individual, shook my friend's hand, stating that now "they could all be friends." We discuss the topic of abnormal aggression later in the chapter.

CLASSIFICATION OF AGGRESSION

Not surprisingly, because aggression is a complex behavior, it has received multiple classifications throughout the years. But research using animals suggests that there are at least two types of aggression. The first, called *defensive aggression*, comprises aggressive acts performed by animals in response to a stimulus perceived as threatening by the animal. In animals, acts of defensive aggression are frequently accompanied by signs of rage, such as raising of hair, lowering of tail, and growling. The second type of aggression, *predatory aggression*, consists of acts performed to fulfill a need, such as feeding or establishing territory limits. Signs of rage do not usually accompany predatory acts. This distinction between defensive and predatory aggression is more than just descriptive; recent research suggests that different circuits in the brain are responsible for each type.

The matter of aggression is much more complex in humans, but there appear to be certain parallel between defensive and predatory aggression in animals and reactive and proactive aggression in humans. *Reactive aggression* refers to acts committed in response to a stimulus initiated by another individual and perceived as threatening by the first. Acts of reactive aggression are therefore defensive acts. *Proactive aggression*, on the other hand, comprises acts of aggression performed because they are necessary to achieve a certain goal other than defense. The motive for proactive aggression is frequently not clear, but some investigators have suggested that it may represent an evolutionary carryover from the time when aggressive acts were necessary to obtain nourishment and fulfill other needs.

THE BRAIN AND AGGRESSION

The performance of an aggressive act involves a complex array of motor, sensory, and behavioral functions, and therefore it implicates a large number of areas of the brain. However, as has become clear in recent years, there are areas in the brain that are specific for coordinating all the behaviors involved in carrying out an aggressive act. This has been discovered because electrically stimulating these areas through means of electrodes placed surgically in the brain causes an animal to become aggressive for the duration of the stimulation. Conversely, destroying these areas of the brain mitigates or suppresses acts of aggression. These areas have mostly been identified in animals, since most experiments have been performed in rats, cats, and nonhuman primates, but there is significant evidence that similarly located areas are present in humans. Moreover, it appears that these aggression areas of the brain are responsible for specific aspects of the aggressive act. Although perhaps guilty of oversimplification, we can divide the functions of these areas as follows:

1. Certain areas of the brain are responsible for the initiation of aggression. These areas are located in the brainstem, hypothalamus, and paralimbic areas. Electrically stimulating these areas brings about aggressive acts, including facial and body display of aggression, as well as frank attacks. Destroying these areas suppresses or mitigates aggression.

2. Certain areas of the brain, when stimulated, suppress or mitigate aggression. For example, stimulating certain areas of the hypothalamus suppresses a normally aggressive responses of male monkeys to other males (thus, the hypothalamus has areas responsible for initiating aggression and other areas for suppressing aggression).

3. Certain areas of the brain are responsible for modulating an aggressive response so that it is appropriate to the particular circumstance. These areas appear to direct the areas responsible for initiating and suppressing aggression, creating a balance between the two so that the response is appropriate to the particular circumstance. Examples of these areas are the amygdala and the frontal lobes.

    The amygdala is a fascinating area of the brain that is located in the region of the temporal lobes. Although it has a number of functions, it seems that one of its most important roles is to link information received by all of the senses (including visual, auditory, and sensory information) with all that is known about that information. For example, the amygdala links the visual information received by the occipital of the image of a friend with all that is known about that friend. It then imparts affective coloring, that is, it ties the image to the perception of a certain emotion or feeling. Thus, the amygdala has access to a wide array of information acquired by the individual through past experience.

    In regard to aggression, the amygdala has a very important role: It ties a certain image of an object or person with the "feeling" it has about that object. For example, certain species of monkey normally react aggressively toward human beings. We could argue that schematically, the visual areas of the monkey brain send the image to the amygdala, which then ties the image with all it knows about human beings, including that they are not likable creatures. It then directs areas of the brain responsible for initiating aggression to attack the human. Monkeys in which the amygdalas have been surgically destroyed fail to respond in an aggressive fashion, because the image of the human is not linked by the amygdala with the monkey's feelings of dislike for humans. In fact, a strange situation arises if only one amygdala is destroyed. If we were to draw a vertical line at the level of our nose, we could divide our world in two. Each amygdala receives information about only one of the two halves. If a human approaches a monkey from the side connected with the destroyed amygdala, the monkey reacts in a friendly fashion. If it approaches the monkey from the side connected with the intact amygdala, the monkey reacts aggressively.

Humans who have damage to their amygdalas resulting from infections, tumors, or surgical lesions also become less aggressive. Objects or persons that previously evoked angry or aggressive responses fail to evoke a similar response. In fact, patients become more apathetic toward the external world. They fail to link objects or people with past feelings about them, thus dulling their response to them.

Conversely, the electrical stimulation of the amygdala due to epilepsy brings about the opposite response. People thus afflicted become more emotional during the epileptic attack, frequently becoming more religious or preoccupied with moral issues.

Other areas of the brain that play an important role in the modulation of aggression in such a way that its expression is appropriate to the particular circumstance and the social norm are the frontal lobes. This seems to be true in both reactive and proactive aggression. The frontal lobes, as described in prior sections, act as the "black box" between a stimulus and a response. In the case of reactive aggression, the stimulus consists of a provocation from the outside world. In proactive aggression, the stimulus is an aggressive impulse from within an individual. Upon receipt of that stimulus, the frontal lobes consider and analyze a large amount of data, including past knowledge and experience, circumstances surrounding the present event, and the available options. They then decides upon an action strategy. As we discuss later, damage to the frontal lobes has been implicated in some aggressive individuals.

4. Finally, certain areas appear to be responsible for initiating or suppressing specific types of aggression. These areas have been identified in animals but not in humans. For example, much scientific evidence related to animals suggests that defensive and predatory types of aggression are performed by two different systems and neuronal pathways in the brain. Interrupting one of the circuits eliminates one type of aggression, leaving the other one intact. Such circuits have been well identified in rats, cats, and other species. There is also some evidence that neuronal groups and pathways responsible for each type of aggression in these animals utilize specific neurotransmitters.

ABNORMAL AGGRESSION

As discussed, the line between a normal and an abnormal aggressive act is a fine one. This is an area that requires much deliberation, but for the purpose of our discussion, abnormal acts of aggression meet two criteria. One, they exceed those acts needed to fulfill a survival goal. Two, the behavioral act ranges outside the norm for the particular species, culture, and circumstance. That is, a normal individual faced with the same circumstances and opportunity would not commit a comparable aggressive act.

In keeping with our previous classification of aggression, abnormal aggressive acts can also be grouped into two categories. In abnormal reactive aggression, an individual has an excessive or aberrant aggressive response to a stimulus that would normally evoke some or predictable anger in most people. This type of act is a disinhibited and out-of-proportion reaction to a situation. The individual fails to inhibit his response so that it is in line with the particular circumstance. An example clarifies this concept: A patient of mine, a short-statured, normally nonviolent individual who became significantly disinhibited after a traumatic brain injury, was involved in a physical altercation in a bar after a tall, muscular individual called him "Shorty." My patient reacted to the insult "without thinking" by striking the other individual, who then proceeded to beat up my patient. In his account of the event a few days later, my patient admitted he had reacted too quickly, without considering that the other individual was intoxicated and much larger than himself. When he realized this, it was too late. Any "normal" individual would have become annoyed at being called Shorty but would have considered a number of factors (including size of the aggressor) and would have inhibited his "natural" or automatic response to strike the other individual. In reactive aggression, a person frequently feels remorseful after the event, often claiming that he was unable to control his aggressive reaction. This is often the case with child and spouse abusers.

Reactive aggression is often associated with damage to the brain, especially with lesions to the frontal lobes such as occur in patients with traumatic brain injury. A significant proportion of patients with reactive aggression often have a history of being victims of aggression while in their youth. They frequently display mild abnormalities in their neurological exams and neurological tests such as electroencephalograms. Some investigators have suggested that victims of aggression during childhood suffer physical trauma to the brain, later resulting in aggressive behavior.

Patients emerging from coma after suffering a number of diverse injuries to the brain frequently display this reactive aggression. This reaction is frequently seen even in individuals who are normally peaceful, law-abiding citizens. The aggressive response disappears once the patient becomes more conscious and aware of himself and his surroundings. This has led some investigators to theorize that reactive aggression is a default mechanism, perhaps a defensive response of the brain that is normally inhibited by the cortex. Loss of cortical activity such as occurs in coma results in failure to inhibit this aggressive stand. Similarly, any factors that interfere with cortical activity, such as alcohol and drugs, affect this inhibition and result in reactive aggression. Indeed, many of the aggressive activities in the United States have been associated with the concomitant use of alcohol or drugs.

The second type of abnormal aggression, proactive aggression, refers to acts of aggression that are either means to an end or ends themselves. The mechanisms underlying proactive aggression are poorly understood. The person committing such acts is not reacting uncontrollably to a stimulus but is deliberately committing the aggressive act. Such acts are frequently premeditated, planned, or at least foreseen. Cultural factors are extremely important in proactive aggression. For example, certain cultures tolerate or even encourage aggressive acts toward certain ethnic, racial, or religious groups or one gender (typically females). Certain gangs promote frequent, random aggression as an initiation rite.

Acts of proactive aggression are committed by what society frequently labels as sociopathic individuals. The aggressive act can be a means to an end, such as killing people in order to rob them, or as an end itself because such individuals enjoy the aggressive act itself or the pain inflicted upon other individuals. This is frequently the case in habitual killers.

Even though this classification of aggression has some use, there is significant overlap between it and reactive aggression. First, both types are frequently encountered in aggressive individuals, although one of the two types tends to predominate. Learning and cultural factors are also important to both. Thus, certain cultures may encourage reactive aggression, frequently in a selective fashion. Many cultures tolerate or encourage reactive aggression to women or children. Selective proactive aggression is also encouraged and tolerated in certain cultural groups, such as aggression geared toward certain racial, ethnic, or religious groups.

WHY ARE SOME INDIVIDUALS MORE AGGRESSIVE THAN OTHERS?

This is an extremely difficult question to answer, but many theories have been advanced.

The *genetic* basis of aggression, that is, explaining differences in aggression between individuals from a genetic perspective, is an extremely controversial topic. Clearly, genetics are important in aggression in certain nonhuman species. Certain breeds of dogs, for example, are more aggressive than other breeds, a fact that can have only genetic causes. In fact, careful selective breeding of aggressive individuals within a certain species, such as guard dogs or fighting cocks, is a technique commonly utilized by breeders who want aggressive animals.

The issue is far from clear in humans. Certain cultures, such as certain Amazon tribes are more aggressive than others, but it is extremely difficult to factor out learning and cultural issues as causes for that aggression. However, some studies have shown that individuals with certain chromosomal abnormalities are overrepresented; for example, they are more highly represented in prison populations. Other studies have claimed that the monozygotic (or identical) twins born of aggressive individuals are also overly aggressive.

The role of *learning* in aggression is another controversial issue that would take several volumes to discuss. Here we limit ourselves to pointing out that learning results in structural changes in the brain, as discussed in the section on brain plasticity. It is entirely possible—and likely—that individuals exposed to aggression, especially early in life, undergo certain structural changes in the brain that cause them to be more aggressive. This is a very important topic, considering the display of aggression to which humans are constantly exposed in the media. Supporting the role of learning and exposure in aggression is strong evidence that a very large proportion of adults who have committed an aggressive act have a history of having been exposed to or been the victims of violence in their early youth.

The role of *brain abnormalities* in aggression is another area that has received much attention. Numerous studies have shown that subtle abnormalities in various tests of neurological function are more frequent in aggressive than in nonaggressive individuals. However, there is so much conflicting scientific data on the subject that it is very difficult to interpret. Another confusing variable is that the abnormalities found point to many different areas of the brain. Clouding this issue even further is the fact that aggressive individuals are also more likely to suffer neurological damage, since they are more likely to be involved in activities that can result in such damage. Whether brain damage results in aggression or vice versa is difficult to ascertain.

That being said, certain lesions in the brain result in increased aggression. As discussed, a significant proportion of patients who suffer traumatic brain injury and as a result suffer trauma to the frontal lobes become more aggressive. These patients classically display increased reactive aggression, presumably because they lack frontal lobe function to modulate the appropriate display. Lesions in other areas of the brain, such as tumors in the base and the limbic and paralimbic areas of the brain, also have resulted in increased aggression in some patients.

Considering what we discussed about the aggressive areas of the brain, increased aggression could theoretically result from an overactivity of areas that initiate aggression, underactivity of areas that decrease aggression, or malfunction of areas that modulate aggression. Our present state of knowledge does not allow us to make any valid conclusions about this issue.

The role of *neurotransmitters* in aggression is another topic that has received much attention because of its possible implications for treatment. For example, levels of serotonin in the brain have been found to be lower in some individuals who commit violent rather than nonviolent suicides. Some investigators have suggested that serotonin may have a mitigating effect on aggression. Conversely, some data suggests that drugs that affect the dopaminergic system, such as amphetamines and cocaine, can make certain individuals more aggressive. On the other hand, drugs that decrease the actions of dopamine, such as neuroleptics, have a calming effect on agitated individuals. This suggests a role for dopamine in aggression.

Hormones, especially testosterone, also have an important role in aggression in both animals and humans. For example, dominant male rats have a higher blood level of testosterone than do submissive animals. In humans, studies performed in children have shown that boys with increased testosterone are more likely to be aggressive and to display low tolerance to frustration. Violent criminals are also more likely to have high testosterone levels, as are alcoholics who abuse other people. The use of steroids for body-building purposes also increase the level of aggression. Further support for the role of hormones in aggression is provided by research that suggests that aggressive women are more likely to commit aggressive acts during premenstrual periods.

II Interaction Between Body and Brain

Recently I heard this anecdote: An army general, a highly revered national hero, was being interviewed by a reporter while waiting to go into battle, mounted on his white steed. His faithful troops waited behind him.

"General," said the reporter, "The fate of the nation is dependent on this battle, and all eyes are looking to you. But I have a question. Why is it that you wear a red jacket when going into battle?"

"There is a distinct reason, my son," answered the general. "When I ride my horse onto the battlefield, there is a high probability that I may be wounded. If that were to happen, my troops would be dismayed at the sight of my blood, and I fear that this may have a negative impact on their fighting. I wear a red jacket because its color will conceal my blood."

The reporter nodded with admiration at the general's courage. Suddenly a soldier approached them, shouting, "General, the enemy is rapidly approaching and their number is much larger than we anticipated. Should I bring you your red jacket in preparation for battle?"

The general gazed at the enemy and quietly answered, "Yes, but today also bring me my brown pants."

This story provides an example of the interaction between the brain and the gastrointestinal system. All of us have experienced how feelings and emotions such as anger, fear, anxiety, love, and hate influence the body's functions, including blood pressure, heart rate, degree of sweating, and yes, even gastrointestinal functions. This interaction between the brain and organs of the body is key to our survival, and it also can be very powerful, which explains why certain excessive emotional states such as fear or anger can result in a person suffering a fatal heart attack.

As with all other functions of the brain, certain areas of the brain are specifically involved in the control of the body's functions. There are two types of areas. The first are those that have direct impact upon the body's system; that is, their activity involves acting upon such systems or receiving information from them. Other areas act as the intermediaries between the brain and the body, as we will discuss.

The chief area representing the first type is the hypothalamus, a small nucleus located at the base of the brain. The hypothalamus is the chief of operations for the brain's control over bodily functions. It controls the body's functions by means of two systems: a wired and a wireless one. The former consists of the endocrinologic system, the latter the autonomic system. Both are discussed in this chapter. In addition to the hypothalamus, other areas located in the spinal cord, brainstem, cerebellum, and cortex are also capable of modifying the body's functions by acting upon the ANS and the neuroendocrinologic system.

Other areas of the brain, such as the limbic and paralimbic areas, act as the intermediaries or mediators between the brain and body, providing that elusive connection between body and mind, or the physical and the mental. These areas are extensively connected with both the brain cortex and the brain areas directly responsible for control of the body's functions, such as the hypothalamus. They thus direct or inform the hypothalamus about the prevailing mental state, so that it can act accordingly. Additionally, since they also receive information from the hypothalamus, they are able to inform the cortex about the prevailing physical state. The mind and the body do not act independently of each other.

THE AUTONOMIC NERVOUS SYSTEM

The ANS is a complex system of neurons connected on one end with various areas of the brain, including the hypothalamus, spinal cord, brainstem, and limbic and paralimbic areas, as well as other areas of the brain. On the other end, the ANS is connected with most of the body's organs, including the heart, blood vessels, sweat glands, gastrointestinal system, kidneys, bladder, and virtually all other areas. The ANS carries information both ways, from the organs to the brain and vice versa. It thus carries information about the organs to the brain, and information about the brain to the organs.

Most of the organs of the body are able to function to some degree without input or control from the brain. Indeed, in experiments in which the ANS is disconnected from the body's organs, the heart keeps beating, the gastrointestinal system keeps digesting food, and so on with other organs. For example, if the nerves going from the brain to the heart by means of the ANS were cut, causing a disconnection between heart and brain, the heart would continue to beat in a relatively normal fashion. However, activities originating in the brain, such as emotions, would have no effect on heart rate.

In fact, most of your organs function much of the time on "automatic pilot." This is definitely in your best interest. Just think what your day would be like if on top of everything else you have on your mind, you needed to worry about maintaining blood pressure, regulating your body's temperature, controlling immunity, or all of the thousands of functions the brain does. Therefore, most of the brain's functions run on automatic pilot, without you having to worry about them at all times. That is why when people tell me that they have a lot on their mind, I raise my index finger and remind them how thankful they should be about the fact that much of the brain runs on automatic pilot. For some reason, however, all I get when I say this are puzzled looks, and most people fail to appreciate the wisdom of my statement.

However, the organs' only connection with what's happening outside of the body is the brain; that is, the heart or blood vessels have no connection with the eyes or other receptors that receive information from the outside world. It is the brain that can process and transmit that information to all of the organs.

There are thus three reasons for the body's control over the other organs by way of the ANS. The first is to keep the organs informed about situations occurring outside the body and thus instructing them to adjust their activity in accordance with certain needs. For example, a person encountering a dangerous situation needs to run away from it. To do so successfully, the heart needs to pump faster and provide more blood for the muscles, the lungs need to provide more oxygen, and so on. The organs have no connection or awareness of situations occurring outside the body and thus require the brain to inform, direct, and coordinate their activities, allowing the body to respond appropriately to situations demanding action.

The second reason is to keep the organs informed about situations occurring in the other organs of the body and to adapt accordingly when the demands arise. For example, a person jogging requires a greater supply of blood to the muscles of the legs, which means that the heart needs to pump more blood and the spleen needs to contract to provide a greater supply of blood. All of this activity is coordinated by the ANS.

The third reason for the brain's control of the internal organs through its action over the ANS is interesting. All emotional states—anger, fear, or love—are accompanied by a number of physical manifestations, including changes in blood pressure, heart rate, degree of sweating, and so on. By means of the ANS, the brain thus gives a physicality to a mental activity. It can even be argued that the physical response is not an accompaniment to the mental emotional state but that it is in itself part of the emotion, inseparable from the mental feeling. An emotion thus has a mental and a physical component; emotions are lived or experienced by both your brain and your body.

Is it possible to have one without the other? The answer to this question is not clear. Some scientist hold that in experimental conditions in which the ANS is disconnected from the brain through means of surgical or pharmacological techniques, it is still possible to feel an emotion, that is, the mental component without the associated physical element, but the intensity of the emotion is decreased.

Other investigators hold that the two components of an emotion are inseparable and have used this theory to their advantage in the treatment of many disorders. For example, anxiety is accompanied by increases in a number of bodily manifestations, including heart rate and blood pressure. A person taught to decrease blood pressure and pulse rate by meditation or biofeedback techniques is able to curb the feeling of anxiety. Similarly, medications that decrease blood pressure have been found to decrease anxiety to a certain degree. On the other hand, medications that decrease anxiety by acting on the brain, such as Valium, also decrease the elevated blood pressure and heart rate that accompany anxiety.

The ANS is made up of two components or systems: the parasympathetic and sympathetic systems. We have already discussed that the functions of the brain are the result of two opposing but complementary forces; for example, movement is the result of the simultaneous actions of antagonistic and agnostic muscles. To a large degree, the same holds true for the ANS. In the case of blood pressure and heart rate, for example, the activation of the parasympathetic component decreases blood pressure and heart rate, while activity of the sympathetic component results in the opposite effect. A balance of the two systems working in harmony and unison results in the appropriate degree of blood pressure and heart rate. In some organ systems, however, such as the gastrointestinal tract, the activity of one system, the parasympathetic, seems to predominate.

Considering the stretch association between the brain and the body's organs through ANS, it is not surprising that the many disorders affecting the brain also affect the function of vital organs of the body. For example, any sudden damage to the brain such as that which occurs in stroke and brain injury can bring about life-threatening changes in such functions such as blood pressure, and cardiac function. Tumors in the brain, especially in areas such as the limbic and paralimbic areas and the hypothalamus, can result in similar bodily changes. Diseases of the brain, such as Parkinson's disease, are accompanied by changes in many bodily functions.

Certain psychiatric conditions, such as generalized anxiety disorder and panic disorders, in which a patient suffers from a mental feeling of anxiety accompanied by increased heart rate, gastrointestinal motility, and sweating, have been attributed in some patients to "overactivity" of certain areas of the brain, such as the paralimbic and limbic areas.

This inseparable association between brain and body explains the association between psychological and physical phenomena. For example, stress, that word so commonly encountered in our current society, is like any other emotional state. It is lived by both the brain and the body.

THE NEUROENDOCRINOLOGIC SYSTEM

Another mechanism by which the brain controls many bodily functions is the neuroendocrinologic system. The body contains a number of glands that regulate many vital functions of our bodies. It is beyond the scope of this manual to describe all glands in detail, but metabolism, growth, sexual function, reproduction, internal homeostasis, and lactation are among the many functions controlled by means of chemical substances called *hormones*, which are manufactured by various glands.

The brain controls most of the endocrine glands of the body through a somewhat hierarchical system. The brain exercises its influence over the hypothalamus, which in turn directs the secretion of a number of hormones by the pituitary gland, often referred to as the chief gland of the body. The pituitary is located at the base of the brain, and it can be divided into an anterior and a posterior component.

Hormones are chemical substances that are manufactured by an endocrine gland and are then released into the bloodstream, which transports them to the specific effector organ, that is, the organ on which they will have an effect.

The pituitary secretes four type of hormones as follows:

1. Hormones that have a role in sexual function, reproduction and maternal lactation. Examples of these include oxytocin, responsible for causing uterine contraction during pregnancy and milk ejection in the mammary glands during breast feeding, and gonadotropin-releasing hormone (GnRH), leutinizing hormone (LH), and follicle-stimulating hormone (FSH), which regulate menstruation as well as other sexual and reproductive functions in both males and females.
2. Hormones that have a role in metabolism. Some examples of releasing factors and their subsequent hormones are thyroid-releasing hormone (TRH), thyroid-stimulating hormone (TSH), corticotropic-releasing hormone (CRH), and adrenocorticotropic hormone (ACTH).
3. Hormones that have a role in the maintenance of internal homeostasis. Such is the case with antidiuretic hormone (ADH).
4. Hormones that have a role in growth. An example is growth-stimulating factor.

How does the hypothalamus regulate the amount of hormone that will be secreted by the pituitary? There appear to be four mechanisms (Figure 11-1):

1. The secretion of hormones in response to electrochemical signals proceeding from neurons in the body. The typical example is the secretion of oxytocin (a hormone that stimulates production and secretion of milk in the mammary glands) in response to an infant's sucking at its mother's breast. Impulses from the nipple of the mother travel to her hypothalamus, which arranges for the immediate secretion of oxcytocin. This entire loop takes place within a few seconds.
2. The secretion of hormones in response to electrochemical impulses proceeding from the cortex. The typical example is the secretion of oxytocin by the mother when she hears her infant crying. The sounds travel to the mother's brain and from there to her hypothalamus. This process can also lead to inhibition of hormonal secretion. For example, severe psychological stress can decrease the secretion of oxytocin (and therefore of milk) in the mother. Severe stress has also

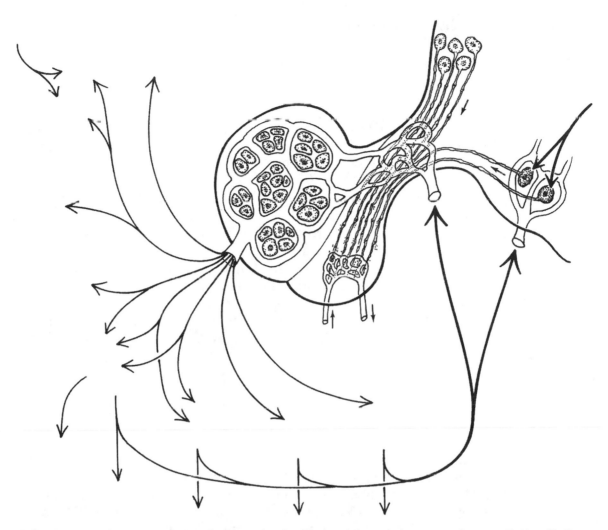

FIGURE 11-1 The pituitary gland receives instructions from the hypothalamus. It then secretes hormones that travel in the bloodstream to other glands of the body.

been known to decrease the secretion of a number of hormones, including those involving menstrual and sexual function and even growth.

3. The secretion or inhibition of secretions of hormones in response to certain conditions existing in the body, such as decreased sodium in the blood, which cells in the hypothalamus itself are able to detect. The hypothalamus contains cells that have sensors able to detect changes in many constituents in the blood, such as sodium and glucose abnormalities. The hypothalamus responds by secreting or inhibiting the secretion of antidiuretic hormone to correct the situation.

4. The secretion or inhibition of hormones in response to the amount of other hormones present in the blood. This is a typical feedback mechanism. For example, the presence of large amounts of thyroid hormone (produced by the thyroid gland) inhibits the secretion of

thyroid-stimulating hormone (produced by the pituitary and resulting in increased activation of the thyroid). This feedback mechanism exists for virtually all hormones. All of the glands of the body send back messages to the pituitary to indicate the need for an increase or decrease in the hormones that it secretes.

An important aspect of the neuroendocrine system is that many areas of the cortex have receptors for hormones. This could explain, at least in part, the changes in mood that certain women experience at various times during the menstrual cycle.

Because of the close connection between the body and the endocrinological system, it is not difficult to understand how conditions that affect the brain can affect the hormonal system. As with the ANS, certain lesions in the brain, such as traumatic brain injury, strokes, and infections, can affect growth, metabolism, internal homeostasis, and sexual function. For example, traumatic brain injury is frequently accompanied by decreased libido in both sexes as well as menstrual alterations in women. Similarly, emotional states can frequently affect hormonal status. For example, severe stress levels can affect growth as well as sexual and reproductive functions.

BRAIN CONTROL

Perhaps one of the most interesting questions that arise from the mind/body interaction is the following: Many of the functions of the body are under control of the brain, but how many of those functions are under our *voluntary* control? That is, can we willingly control our blood pressure, heart rate, degree of sweating, or gastrointestinal motility? Can we control our feelings of thirst, hunger, or cold? Do we have control over our glands? The mind's dominion over the body is a fascinating topic that has been of interest to humankind for thousands of years and has been examined by theologians, philosophers, and psychologists, among many others. Several volumes could be dedicated to its discussion; we touch on the subject briefly here.

If we consider all of the brain functions, we can see that they differ in the degree to which they are under our voluntary control. Some are under a great deal of voluntary control, others are less so, and most of them are somewhat in the middle. We can explore this fascinating subject by referring to Figure 11-2. Three areas can be identified in the figure. Area 1 represents functions, such as language, which are totally under our will. We can thus choose when to speak and when not to speak, as well as determining what to say. Area 3 represents functions that are totally out of our control, such as dreaming. We cannot choose when to dream or not to dream, nor can we choose the content of our dreams. Area 2 represent functions that are somewhat in the middle, having both a volitional and nonvolitional component. Many of the brain's roles in the functions of the

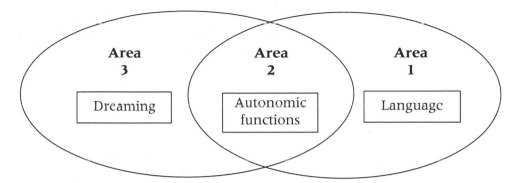

FIGURE II-2   Schematic representation of brain functions and volitional control.

body are in area 2. However, much of the body's function can be brought under voluntary control, albeit in a limited fashion and for a limited amount of time. For example, utilizing certain modalities such as relaxation techniques and biofeedback, individuals can learn to modify their blood pressure, pulse, degree of sweating, temperature, and gastrointestinal motility. The practical value of these modalities in treating clinical problems such as high blood pressure or gastrointestinal disorders remains disputed, and more research needs to be conducted. Some of the limitations of these techniques are obvious; even if we are able to voluntarily control our blood pressure, it would be impossible to continuously attend to this task because it would require our permanent attention.

Learning and practice certainly have a role in voluntary modulation of the body's functions. Thus, certain groups involved in rigorous meditation practices, such as Buddhist monks, develop a remarkable ability to regulate a number of the body's functions.

THE BRAIN AND IMMUNITY

Immunity refers to the process by which your body fights off infections. Your body is in a constant state of alert and warfare. At all times it is being invaded by billions of organisms, including viruses, bacteria, and parasites. The system in your body responsible for defending you from these invaders is called the *immune system*, and it consists of an extremely sophisticated protection mechanism that would put the Pentagon to shame. This system includes formidable walls to prevent enemy infiltration, mechanisms for surveillance, collection of intelligence information, enemy recognition, storage of information about the enemy in case of future attack, and a wide array of extremely sophisticated weaponry for isolating and destroying the enemy.

Like any sophisticated defense system, the immune system has a coordinating entity, and research has evidenced that the brain may play a large role in directing the efforts of the immune system. However, the mechanisms by which the brain affects immunity are poorly understood.

We do know that many disorders that involve the brain affect immunity. Such is the case of psychiatric disorders. Patients suffering from depression have abnormalities in their immunological response to infections. Psychological factors such as bereavement also affect immunity.

One of the most fascinating proofs for the role of the brain on immunity lies in what's called the *placebo effect*. Experimental treatment trials frequently divide patients into three groups; one gets the real experimental drug, the second one gets a placebo (such as sugar pills), and the third group gets no treatment. Invariably, the placebo groups show some improvement, which sometimes is very significant. Other treatment modalities, such as the use of imagining techniques in the treatment of various disorders, although scientifically unproven, point toward the role of the brain on immunity.

Certainly, various components of the immune system receive input from the brain through means of the autonomic and neuroendocrinologic system. Lymphocytes, blood cells that have a prominent role in immunity, have been found to have receptors for neurotransmitters, although their role in the immune process is not well understood.

12 Disorders That Can Affect Your Brain

The brain can be the site of many types of lesion, as described in this chapter.

VASCULAR LESIONS

For brain cells to grow, prosper and perform their jobs, they need a ready supply of nutrients and fuel. In addition, waste, which is a byproduct of cell activity, must also be removed constantly to prevent it from becoming toxic to cells. A dependable transport system to both transport nutrients and remove waste is an absolute necessity. The blood provides such as system. It courses through the body on "roads" called blood vessels.

The brain is a ravenous consumer of nutrients. As discussed in the chapter on nutrition, it accounts for less than 2 percent of a person's weight, yet it consumes 20 percent of the body's energy. Brain cells have additional characteristics that differentiate them from other cells in the body. First, neurons are unable to use any other fuel but glucose; second, they are unable to store any significant amount of glucose within themselves. Finally, unlike other cells, neurons are unable to function for any significant amount of time without oxygen. Because of this strong dependence of the brain on glucose and oxygen, interruption of blood flow to the brain results in neuronal death within six to eight minutes. The most common reasons for occlusion of blood vessels are plaques. Infarcts, or strokes as they are commonly known, result from the occlusion of a blood vessel, which interrupts the blood flow to a particular area of the brain. Occlusion of vessels can occur at many different levels; therefore, strokes can affect multiple areas of the brain, the number and location of which determine the resulting neurological deficit.

Hemorrhages, on the other hand, result from the bursting of a blood vessel, which causes the *extravasation* of blood—the spilling of blood into the brain matter. Again, the areas of the brain affected and the resulting neurological deficits depend on the blood vessel involved.

INFECTIOUS DISORDERS

An infection is an invasion by foreign agents. The body is in a constant state of war, perpetually fighting off invasions by a number of organisms such as bacteria, viruses, and parasites. Infection of the brain can occur via multiple mechanisms, but before invading the brain, organisms must be able to gain access to it, which by itself is a formidable task. As discussed in prior sections, the brain is protected from the outside by a number of "walls," including the skull and the blood/brain barrier.

Organisms can access the brain via several mechanisms. Organisms in the blood can penetrate the brain by finding or fabricating leaks in the blood/brain barrier. They can also access the brain by penetrating the skull, such as occurs in the transmission of infection from the sinuses or the inner ear to the brain. Also, it is thought that certain viruses can enter the brain through the nose.

Once in the brain, organisms can create havoc in many ways, but the net result is the death or damage of neurons and/or glial cells. The degree of damage can vary widely, ranging from frank death to damage resulting in neuronal inability to transmit information. Thus, certain organisms can harm a neuron in such a way that it appears morphologically normal to the electron microscope, and yet the cell becomes unable to depolarize in response to stimulation by other neurons.

Some organisms have a predilection for certain areas of the brain. Certain organisms attacking the covering of the brain (the meninges) result in *meningitis*. Others prefer the brain cells themselves (which results in encephalitis), and yet others attack certain brain cells preferentially. For example, the herpes virus, which can produce a devastating infection, specifically attacks cells in the temporal and other limbic structures. Infected individuals who survive are left with prominent behavioral and cognitive deficits, since limbic areas are involved in these functions.

Special mention must be made of viruses, which are cunning invaders. They penetrate a neuron using a variety of mechanisms. Once inside the cell, they take over the cell's manufacturing system, forcing it to fabricate more viruses until the cell virtually dies from exhaustion. Newborn viruses then leave the cell to invade other cells and begin the process all over again.

AUTOIMMUNE DISORDERS

As stated, the body is in a constant state of alert and defense against invading organisms. The system responsible for this defense is called the *immune system*, which consists of a formidable mechanism of defense comprising a number of systems. Unfortunately, this same immune system can turn upon the same body that it is supposed to defend. The reason for this "mistake" is unknown, but it results in what are called *autoimmune disorders*, in which the immune system mistakes certain cells or components of cells as foreign and attacks them.

Various components of the brain can be the seat of autoimmune disorders. Neurons, glial cells, and cerebral blood vessels can be attacked by the body's immune system and succumb to its injury. This occurs in certain diseases such as Lupus disease or Sjogren syndrome. Multiple sclerosis is thought to have an autoimmune basis.

DEMYELINATING DISORDERS

Myelin is the insulating material that surrounds axons and is manufactured by specialized glial cells called oligodendrocytes. When a disease process affects myelin, the capacity of an axon to transmit electrical impulses is severely hampered.

Myelin is the frequent seat of autoimmune disorders. The immune system mistakenly interprets myelin as a foreign invader and destroys it. Such is the case after a particular infection in which the infecting organisms have some molecular similarity with myelin. In this case, the immune system manufactures antibodies, or "missiles," specifically aimed at the infecting organisms. Unfortunately, these same antibodies then attack normal myelin because of its similarity to the invading organism. The same situation can occur with vaccinations in rare cases. The vaccine can contain a certain molecule with a similarity to myelin. The resulting immune response the vaccine brings on then attacks the body's myelin. Fortunately, these situations are extremely rare.

The most common demyelinating disorder is multiple sclerosis, a disease that affects mylein in the brain and spinal cord and which can have severe consequences in brain function.

NEOPLASMS

Neoplasms occur from the growth of cells that originate from within the body itself. The reason cells become neoplastic at a particular time is not well understood, although a number of reasons, including genetic and environmental factors, have been implicated in some types of neoplasm. Neoplasm in the brain can originate from cells in the brain itself or can originate in other areas of the brain and be transported to the brain, where it grows. The latter type is called *brain metastasis*. Neoplastic cells differ in degree of similarity to normal brain cells. Undifferentiated neoplastic cells, for example, have little morphological and functional similarity with normal cells, but differentiated cells can be very similar to normal cells.

Neoplastic cells cause damage by occupying space and crushing other cells around them, by consuming nutrients destined for other cells, by producing waste that is toxic to surrounding cells, and by many other mechanisms.

DEGENERATIVE DISORDERS

Certain specific populations of neurons can be the seat of diseases affecting the brain. In these conditions, those specific neurons progressively become nonfunctional and eventually die.

In many of these conditions, scientists understand what happens but not why it happens. Thus, we know that Parkinson's disease results from the destruction of neurons in the substantia nigra. These neurons are responsible for manufacturing dopamine. The neurological deficits that accompany the disease are the result of a lack of dopamine and can be corrected to a certain extent by the supplementation of dopamine. Huntington's disease also occurs because of destruction of certain populations of neurons in the caudate and other nucleuses, which results in a neurotransmitter imbalance. Alzheimer's disease also preferentially affects certain populations of brain cells that have much to do with cognition. The reason for or cause of this disease is not well understood, although nutritional, toxic, and genetic causes have been implicated.

TOXINS

A number of toxins, too numerous to name, can affect brain cells. Lead, mercury, and manganese, among many, continue to be culprits in many areas of the world, including the United Sates. Certain toxins have a predilection for affecting certain areas of the brain, although most of the brain is affected. Thus, mercury preferentially affects the cerebellum, resulting in problems of balance and coordination. Lead poisoning can result in cognitive problems in both children and adults. It can also specifically affect certain nerves in the body.

TRAUMA

Brain injury resulting from trauma, such as that which occurs from motor vehicle accidents and acts of violence, is one of the most commons neurological disorders in the United States. Research performed in recent years has elucidated the pathophysiological mechanisms responsible for brain damage from trauma. Traumatic brain injury preferentially affects areas of the brain involved in cognition and behavior (the frontal lobe and limbic areas).

NUTRITIONAL DISORDERS

The brain requires a vast supply and variety of nutrients for survival, growth, and normal function, as described in the chapter on nutrition.

Index